MW00961864

SMALL BUSINESS ACCOUNTING
Money Matters Made Easy:
A Beginner's Guide for Entrepreneurs

By Amy York

© **Copyright 2023 Rabbit Hole Publications LLC**
All rights reserved.

The contents of this book may not be reproduced, duplicated or transmitted without direct written permission from the author.

Under no circumstances will any legal responsibility or blame be held against the publisher for any reparation, damages, or monetary loss due to the information herein, either directly or indirectly.

Legal Notice:
This book is copyright protected. This is only for personal use. You cannot amend, distribute, sell, use, quote or paraphrase any part or the content within this book without the consent of the author.

Disclaimer Notice:
Please note the information contained within this document is for educational and entertainment purposes only. Every attempt has been made to provide accurate, up to date and reliable complete information. No warranties of any kind are expressed or implied. Readers acknowledge that the author is not engaging in the rendering of legal, financial, medical or professional advice. The content of this book has been derived from various sources. Please consult a licensed professional before attempting any techniques outlined in this book.

By reading this document, the reader agrees that under no circumstances is the author responsible for any losses, direct or indirect, which are incurred as a result of the use of information contained within this document, including, but not limited to, —errors, omissions, or inaccuracies.

This book may contain affiliate links. If you purchase a product or service through these links, I may receive a small commission at no extra cost to you. All opinions expressed in this book are not influenced by any affiliate relationships.

Get Your Free Gift: An Accounting Checklist

Get your accounting in order with this handy checklist as your guide. No more financial scrambling or disorganization!

Use this list as your recipe for money management success. Tick off key tasks to keep your books fully prepped and expenses accurately measured all year long.

You'll be head chef of your finances, with perfectly organized statements and invoices ready for inspection. Whether you're a beginner or a seasoned money pro, this checklist helps you whip your accounting into shape.

All the ingredients for managing your money matters with ease in one place. Your accounting will rise beautifully and books stay crisp with this checklist. Get ready for your best financial year yet!

The checklist includes:

- **Daily** tasks like checking cash, filing records
- **Weekly** tasks like paying vendors, sending invoices
- **Monthly** tasks like reviewing aging, closing the books
- **Quarterly** tasks like updating forecasts, paying quarterly taxes
- **Annual** tasks like preparing budgets, reviewing year-end reports, plus
- Room for **Notes**

You'll want to use the checklist again and again.

The checklist is free to download and it's available now. To get your copy, simply Scan the QR Code or open the link below:

https://dl.bookfunnel.com/jkjk5nrvta

Table of Contents

CHAPTER 1

Dipping Your Toes in the World of Financial Accounting

Did you know that over 61 percent of small businesses[1] worldwide struggle with cash flow, whereas nearly a third can't pay vendors, loans, themselves, or employees due to cash flow issues? In addition, 82 percent of small businesses[2] and startups fail due to cash flow management. Despite this, over 70 percent of small businesses[3] don't hire an accountant, and 18 percent don't use software[4].

If that sounds like you, you either don't have a penny to spare or believe you don't need an accountant. But that's far from the truth. Good news: you don't need to spend a fortune on hiring an accountant! Instead, you can learn accounting basics to keep track of your assets, income, and cash flow and lead your team. If you're unsure how to start developing accounting skills, *you're not alone!*

Meet Caroline, owner of an increasingly popular sweet-smelling local eatery, "Sweet Caroline Bakery," dedicated to making mouthwatering desserts and transforming her small business into a prosperous one. But there's one reason her business is stuck: Caroline has *no* insights into her bakery's financial health!

Not only does this hinder her business growth, but it also keeps her from accurately filing taxes and creating cash flow reports. Unable to decipher the figures and jargon dancing on her financial statements and struggling to make the right business decisions, Caroline decided it was time to learn everything about the basics of financial accounting!

Taking the First Step: Why Caroline Wanted to Discover the World of Accounting

Accounting is critical for *every* small business owner. Although most entrepreneurs and business owners dread learning about it, it's essential for evaluating financial performance, empowering decision-making, and creating a clear business picture.

Without the appropriate accounting skill, like Caroline, you'll be drowning under endless stacks of financial documents trying to make sense of your payroll, profits, liabilities, and taxes. Fortunately, you don't need to become an expert in accounting overnight to get your finances in order and your business on track to success!

All you need is to learn the basics of financial accounting. With a few accounting skills in your back pocket, neither you nor Caroline will have to worry about delays in record-keeping or late financial reports that create devastating business setbacks. Instead, by learning to read financial statements and prepare forecasts, Caroline can raise capital for her bakery and continue expanding.

Diving Deep: The Importance of Accounting for Small Businesses

It's time for Caroline to put her accounting skills to the test. They are the only missing link between her upscale bakery dreams and success!

But before we start kneading that dough, let's find out why financial accounting is the secret ingredient to soft, puffy bread. First, we will talk about those dough-lightful reasons for enhancing your accounting skills.

Meet Legal Regulations and Requirements
You wouldn't try baking a new kind of cupcake without following the recipe, so you shouldn't run a business without following state and federal laws.

By keeping financial records and accurate reports, Caroline can stay on the right side of the law and steer clear of legal repercussions. Plus, it saves you from turning your work office upside down during tax season!

Create Accurate Financial Forecasts
Just like you wouldn't try a new recipe without first checking the ingredients; similarly banks, lenders, investors, and stakeholders won't fund a venture without first seeing your financial predictions.

Without this information, Caroline is struggling to find investors and raise capital.

This is why Caroline must rely on accounting information to create insightful financial forecasts, including economic projections, monthly expenditures, and financial statements-something you can't do if you lack a basic understanding!

Curate Effective Budgets
Running a business is like baking a cake; it requires precision and dedication. But without the right ingredients, it is just a recipe for disaster! When setting up a business, budgeting is that essential ingredient that can turn your old family recipe into a hit.

Financial planning is half the battle. Without solid understanding, it is like throwing your dough in the trash. Caroline focuses on financial accounting, which helps her make informed decisions, organize her records, and outline her business expenditures on raw goods, employees, advertising, and marketing.

This means she will avoid stacking extra bags of flour in her pantry and won't be wasting her capital on unnecessary expenses. Learning about financial accounting will allow Caroline to stay on track. So let's start baking with the right skills and knowledge to turn your business into a sweet success!

Unlock Opportunities to Raise Capital

Psst...here is a secret no one will tell you, especially the financial giants—banks and accounting businesses! You need to keep your records straight and up-to-date to get the funding you need for up scaling your business.

An organization without a solid financial plan is like a mystery box full of unknown surprises. While you'll be tempted to unwrap it, you wouldn't want to invest in something risky. Financial bookkeeping defines your commitment and business knowledge to venture capitalists, investors, and bankers.

So no matter how hard Caroline works to create the perfect pastries, she won't find any investors without showcasing her organized bank records.

PS: The key is proper record-keeping to let the investors' money roll in!

Aid in Tracking Cash Flow

Just like it's important to know how much flour you have before you start baking a cake, business owners need to track their cash flow. By tracking your daily cash flow, you can monitor your spending and hit short-term goals with minimum panic attacks.

If the word *how?* is bouncing around your head, don't worry; the answer is right here. Accounting knowledge equips you with the tools to record and interpret financial transactions, so you no longer see only weird squiggles when you pick up your cash flow and income statements. Plus, by mastering accounting, Caroline can make smart budgets that improve her cash flow and ensure that her bakery continues to reign the city!

Determine Profitability
Every business needs to generate profits to flourish. Whether your business can generate high sales revenue or fails to garner sufficient profits can force you to pull the shutter on your business.

For instance, Caroline's cupcake production requires certain ingredients. But if she's spending $1.45 per cupcake and selling it for $2, that accounts for a mere $0.55 profit—which is too low to be sustainable. Overall, learning how your assets drive sales is essential to cover inventory expenses and boost profits!

Besides this, Caroline has to show banks and investors she can repay costs on time by providing this financial info. If she sends in a page full of indecipherable numbers, it's likely no prospect will respond.

Avoid Making Financial Errors
Another excellent reason to learn accounting is to avoid costly financial mistakes; trust us, Caroline had to deal with her fair share of burnt and runny cakes. The last thing Sweet Caroline Bakery needs is incorrect bank statements or uninterested investors!

By knowing the ins and outs of financial accounting, Caroline (and you) can avoid the costly mistakes of overdrafts, budgeting errors, or missing tax deadlines. With the right tools and accounting skills, you can prevent financial mishaps that could spoil your business's recipe for success. Prepare yourself today to whip up a storm in the world of business by testing and trying different financial tools!

File Financial Statements Hassle-Free

While running a business, owners must file their financial statements with the relevant regulatory bodies according to tax filing requirements. But if you lack knowledge in accounting, your income tax return may end up like Caroline's—a scribbled mess with confusing calculations. However, with a deep understanding of her financial statements, Caroline can quickly and easily file taxes and then get back to doing what she loves: baking delicious goodness.

Promote Real-Time Growth

You're bound to get bored if you have to make the same three recipes on a daily basis! But the problem is that Caroline can't expand her business without learning the secrets of cash flow management. While accounting sounds like a foreign language to Caroline, it can help her create solid budgets that will support her as she builds her very own baking empire.

With the tools of accounting, Caroline can craft financial predictions and long-term budgets that make her feel confident in her business investments.

Analyze Key Business and Financial Performance Indicators

One thing they don't teach at culinary school is using the numbers in a financial statement to determine business performance. Learning critical accounting numbers can empower Caroline to make her own financial reports and statements. That way, she can track and measure vital performance indicators that display her business's current performance. In addition, she can create year-end and quarterly reports to identify which of her cupcakes are a hit and which ones need a little more sugar.

Getting Started: The Steps to Get Your Business Finances in Order

Knowing *why* you need to learn accounting isn't enough; you must be proactive. Just like Caroline can't turn her tiny bakery into a success story simply by "reading" about accounting, you can't expand your small business by flipping pages.

Now that you're all set, it's time to put your learning into action. But it all starts with writing your business plan; it's like setting the right temperature for your oven. Here are the key ingredients to cook up a successful business plan and avoid the common pitfalls.

Let's roll up our sleeves and sharpen our knives to get started!

Step # 1: Refine Your Business Idea

If you're still in the initial phase, put on your detective hat and do some research. Scoop out the information from your competitors and industry leaders. Find out what they are doing, what's a hit and what's a miss in their business, and what your customers need.

Identifying the gaps within your niche will help you refine your business plan and bring something special to the table.

Since Caroline already runs her local bakery store and wishes to expand, she can overlook this step.

Step # 2: Determine Your Business Structure

Every baking journey starts with choosing the right ingredients to create a fluffy, mouthwatering cake. In the same vein, choosing the right business legal structure is important for running a successful business, especially since it can affect everything from how you file your taxes and create employee payroll to ways to shoulder liability and bankruptcy.

Just like finding the right recipe is important for a delicious cake, so is choosing the right business model for your company. Here are the options Caroline (and most small business owners) consider when deciding on a business structure:

B Corporation (US)

If you're someone who prioritizes profit and social responsibility, the B-Corp setup is the perfect business type for you. It allows small businesses to focus on social and environmental well-being for public interest and financial gain.

If you're wondering what we're talking about, it simply means that small businesses can focus on their social and environmental mission without needing to rely solely on their shareholders. If that sounds awesome, take a seat because most states require members involved in this business structure to submit annual benefit reports.

C Corporation (US)

The legal business model that boosts the confidence of shareholders and makes them feel that they're calling the shots is the C-Corp. But with great power comes great responsibility as it requires extensive record-keeping and high operational costs.

Therefore, it is ideal for medium to big corporations that are willing to take the plunge. It offers exceptional personal liability protection, so if one of the members decides to board a different ship or jumps off the deck, yours will continue to sail without any turbulence.

S Corporation (US)

This is the cool kid in school who knows how to maneuver his way to leadership. The S-Corp model allows you to handle your profit and losses on the basis of your income while dodging pesky corporate taxes.

But let's not jump the gun here. While it seems a lucrative option with minimal paperwork and taxation, there are other features, such as stringent shareholder policies, to consider.

That's not all! An S-Corp is independent of its shareholders, so even if someone sells off their shares, the business keeps going without a hitch.

(Rethinking your decision now?)

Partnership (US and UK)

Partnerships are the best business structure for two or more people planning to combine their resources, skills, and expertise while sharing business responsibilities. These are beneficial for businesses that need diverse talents, demanding lower regulatory requirements than corporations.

The business structure may be of two types:

- **Limited Partnerships (LP)-** This includes one partner with unlimited liability and others with limited liability. So most members of LPs have limited control over the business and its processes.
- **Limited Liability Partnerships (LLP)-** Unlike LPs, limited liability partnerships involve limited

liability for *every* owner. The business structure helps protect partners from debts against each other.

Limited Liability Corporation (LLC) (US and UK)

Caroline's famous cheesecake brownies are a testimony to the art of amalgamation in the dessert sphere, just like LLCs are in the business world. An LLC is a perfect mesh of business corporation and partnership structure. Your personal liability is limited, and your assets are protected from lawsuits and bankruptcy.

Work with a registered acquisition agent to add more owners to your business. Pass down your profit and losses to your income, enjoy lower taxes, and keep your assets protected.

Limited Company (LTD) (UK)

A limited company is another legal structure commonly used in the UK, owned by the shareholders and run by one or more directors. Like LLC, individuals in an LTD can benefit from business profits without stressing about personal liability.

Furthermore, members of an LTD retain their company profits *only* after paying corporation taxes. In addition, business owners must file annual reports and documents with the HMRC and Companies House.

Sole Proprietorship (US)

A sole proprietorship is a one-man show where you're the only one on stage. While you get all the glory, you also take all of the risks and losses.

The structure is best for those who want to be their own bosses and enjoy complete control over their venture. However, it requires utmost dedication and the willingness to put in the time and effort to make it work—it's all on you.

Setting it up is intended to be simple and intuitive for anyone. But managing your finances can get a bit overwhelming at first, so don't hesitate to consult a financial advisor if you need guidance optimizing it for your business. Moreover, the sole owner of this structure assumes liability, which makes you personally *and* financially responsible for business debts.

Sole Trader (UK)

Sole traders are considered "self-employed," but they still have to register their business with their country's regulatory bodies. In this business structure, used mostly in the UK, individuals must pay income taxes and sometimes National Insurance contributions.

Sole traders are ideal for startups, allowing you to retain all your profits. But the downside of this business structure is you'll be financially and personally liable.

A Quick Comparison

Get ready for the final showdown of the popular business structures. At one end, we have the eco-responsible B-Corp, while on the other end is the super smart S-Corp. But here comes sole proprietorship, leaving the reins in your hands. Who will win this epic battle of the corporate world? Let's find out here as we compare the features and benefits of each model:

Business Structure	Liability	Ownership	Taxes
B Corporation	You are not personally liable	One or more owners	Subject to only corporate taxes
C Corporation	You are not personally liable	One or more owners	Subject to only corporate taxes
S Corporation	You are not personally liable	One or more people but a limit of 100	Subject to only personal taxes

Partnership	You are personally and financially liable unless you choose an LP	Two or more owners	Subject to personal and self-employment taxes except for limited partners
LLC	You are not personally liable	One or more members	Subject to self-employment and personal/corporate taxes
Sole Proprietorship	You are personally and financially liable	One owner	Subject to self-employment and personal taxes
LTD (Limited Company)	You are not personally liable	One or more shareholders	Subject to only corporate taxes
Sole Trader	You are personally and financially liable	One owner and multiple staff members	Subject to taxes and national insurance fees

Since Caroline runs a local bakery, she would prefer a business structure that offers minimum complexity and better flexibility. For instance, she could set up a sole proprietorship, since she's a one-woman team, or an LLC since it offers better liability protection.

But before making the right choice, Caroline has to assess her unique business needs and goals. What structure would you pick in her shoes?

Step # 3: Register Your Startup

Once you've decided which business entity best matches your needs, the next step is to register with the government. To establish an LLC, Caroline would need to brainstorm a catchy and memorable business name and determine her business's purpose since "loves making people smile with yummy desserts" doesn't count as professional!

While choosing your business name, ensure that you don't select one registered by another company or that infringes on another trademark brand. To achieve this in the US, Caroline would leverage the *US Patent and Trademark* Office and the website of her state's Secretary of State. But if you're not located in the US, you'll have to check with your local registration agency.

Step # 4: Obtain Your EIN
Neither Caroline nor any small business can create a business structure without filling out the required forms. You'll have to choose a registered agent, pay a filing fee, and apply for a tax identification number in your country (or wherever you're planning to do business).

No matter your business structure (unless you choose sole proprietorship), you must have a federal tax or employer identification number. In most places, you can submit your application through your government agency's unique online portal for approval within seconds.

Alternatively, you can utilize competent registered agent services to complete these steps faster and more efficiently. Caroline does exactly this by taking advantage of a reliable registration tool.

Step # 5: Get the Appropriate Licenses
It's no secret: Your business needs local, state, and federal licenses to operate and succeed. So, before skipping to the next part, check in with your local government office for licensing info.

Or you can do what Caroline did and talk to an attorney.

Step # 6: Open a Bank Account

One valuable tip to live by is *always* to separate your personal and business finances. The last thing you want is for your car to get towed because of a business mishap!

Once you set up your business structure, open a new business bank account. Before heading to the bank, Caroline ensures she has all the right documents, including business formation information, business license, and tax identification numbers.

You can use this account to pay suppliers and receive customer payments. You can go one step further and secure a business credit card to purchase supplies and pay bills on the go. But if you're afraid you'll overspend on supplies and equipment, don't get a credit card!

Step # 7: Choose the Right Accounting Method

As a small business owner, your next step is determining the ideal accounting method to report monthly and annual expenses and income. Typically, business owners choose between cash and accrual.

If you don't understand what cash and accrual mean, think of them as two different ways of enjoying your favorite cake. Cash accounting is like taking a big bite of the cake right away, savoring the instant sweetness and satisfaction.

On the contrary, accrual accounting is like slowly savoring each layer of the cake, enjoying the depth of flavor and complexity that unfolds with each bite. While both methods sound fantastic, it ultimately depends on personal preference and goals.

Some may prefer the simplicity and immediacy of cash accounting, while others may appreciate the accuracy and long-term view of accrual accounting.

For instance, under the cash method, Caroline can pay and record expenses and income when she receives and pays them. But in the accrual method, she can record it when she earns/incurs her income/expense regardless of when they're received or paid.

Since the cash method will not accurately represent her bakery's performance, Caroline can ensure success by choosing and following the accrual method.

Step # 8: Set up Your Accounting System

Congratulations! You've completed most of the heavy work of setting up a new business. So what's left now? You've already decided on your accounting method, so now you only have to find software that matches your needs. The best way to choose the perfect accounting system is to determine your budget, required features, and goals.

(P.S. Look forward to more on this in an upcoming chapter!)

After that, you'll have to set up your chart of accounts (CoA) to track business accounts and transactions. With this, Caroline can track and visualize her assets, liabilities, equity, income, *and* expenses.

But before Caroline jumps headfirst into the wondrous world of CoA, she needs to be able to create one. Here's how she can whip up her very own chart of accounts.

Setting Account Types

The CoA is to your business finances what flour is to Caroline's cake: Without it, nothing works! So to get started on the way to making smart business decisions, Caroline needs to learn how to set up an account.

Create a Balance Sheet Account

With a balance sheet account, Caroline can stay on top of her business assets, liabilities, and shareholders' equity. But keeping track of this account type means going the extra mile and creating lists of current and intangible assets, current and long-term liabilities, and retained earnings.

(P.S. Don't worry, you'll learn all these new terms in the upcoming chapters.)

Profit and Loss Statement Account

If you didn't figure it out from the name, Caroline uses these types of accounts to track her profits and losses.

By staying up to date with income sources, sales, services, rent, salaries, and office supplies, Caroline ensures that she always has enough to spend on her ingredients.

Using Codes for Account Sub-Types

Just like you can't learn a new cake recipe with a wave of a wand, you can't set up a CoA overnight. But the best way to get started is to use unique numbers for the five primary categories, i.e., asset, liability, equity, income, and expense account.

The purpose? It helps you stay organized. Now that you've learned what a chart of accounts is and how to set one up, let's dive in deeper. Below we can see the example Caroline uses to further understand the intricacies of a CoA:

Account	Category	Sub-Account	Account Number
Balance Sheet Accounts	Assets	Cash on Hand	1001
		Cash in Bank	1002
		Petty Cash	1003
		Accounts Receivable	1004
		Equipment	1005
		Furnitures and Fixtures	1006
		Inventory	1007
	Liabilities	Accounts Payable	2001
		Wages Payable	2002
		Notes Payable	2003
		Taxes Payable	2004
	Equity	Retained Earnings	3001
		Common Stock	3002
		Preferred Stock	3003
Income Statement Accounts	Revenue	Revenue	4001
		Sales Returns and Allowances	4002
		Sales Discounts	4003
	Expenses	Utilities Expense	5001
		Advertising Expense	5002
		Rent Expense	5003
		Depreciation Expense	5004
		Salaries and Wages Expense	5005

Link: https://www.financestrategists.com/accounting/financial-statements/chart-of-accounts/

As Caroline has already learned what balance sheet accounts and profit and loss statement accounts mean at a surface level, the example above makes a little more sense. Try keeping the information next to you as you interpret the example so you can review the definitions. (Plus, if you're still a little uneasy, don't worry; we've got a whole chapter dedicated to learning how balance sheets and income statements create the perfect mix for financial success.)

Now that Caroline has learned the structure and how to set up a CoA account, she's ready to move on to the next step, which is...creating an online presence! Just like making all kinds of delicious treats in your mind doesn't put them on the table, your business can't transform into a success story without actually getting seen. So let's keep moving.

Step # 9: Register Your Website Domain
No online presence means no unlimited growth, especially in today's tech-savvy world. Fortunately, setting up your website and social media pages doesn't take long.

You only need a trustworthy domain name registrar and a domain that matches your business. Caroline kept an open mind and an open Google tab when diving into domain names, which saved her from a mental breakdown when she found that somebody had already taken the one she wanted. If you're not a fan of falling into the rabbit hole that is online searching, you can outsource website domain setup.

Lastly, business owners need to create an online presence using relevant social media sites. Caroline prefers using Instagram, Pinterest, and Facebook to post aesthetic pictures from her bakery and her delicious concoctions.

Since Caroline's expertise is not limited to the kitchen, she can register her website domain in seconds. There are tons of online websites like *GoDaddy.com* that make this a piece of cake. Or if your technical skills are not up to par, you can hire a freelancer from *Upwork* or *Fiverr*.

Step # 10: Schedule Annual Business Meetings

Without a robust business plan, success can be near impossible. So what does Caroline do? She makes time for weekly and annual business meetings, even if her introverted personality makes her dread them.

Ensure you schedule them a month before and decide on the topic to give everyone, and yourself, enough time to prepare.

Now that Caroline has learned the magic recipe to setting up her business structure and account system, she's all set to whisk up perfection and fold in accurate calculations. With the knowledge of the importance of accounting and its basics, she feels confident not to make half-baked decisions!

But before you call yourself an accounting expert, it's important to get your hands in the financial dough. Below are fun and challenging short and long questions to help you test your new knowledge.

(P.S. You'll find five awesome accounting facts at the bottom!)

Test Your Knowledge: Fun Exercises, Examples, and Tips

Questions
Q1. Caroline has always dreamed of running her own bakery, but what do you think are her financial goals for her sweet venture? Is it to become the next celebrity chef, to sell the best cupcakes in town, or simply to earn enough dough to make ends meet and pay off her debts?

Response:

Q2. Now that we have an idea of Caroline's financial goals, what company structure do you think Caroline should choose and why? Should she opt for a sole proprietorship, a partnership, an LLC, a corporation, or a whole new flavor?

Response:

Short Questions

Try to answer the following super simple and straightforward questions in two to three sentences.

Q1. In one sentence, explain the purpose of accounting. (You can re-read the chapter to decide on your answer.)

Response:

Q2. Caroline is setting up her business structure. She chooses an LLC because of its convenience and liability limitation. What should she do next?

Response:

Q3. What are the two types of accounting methods? Explain their differences.

Response:

Q4. Caroline has set up her business model and financial system. The natural step for her is to...?

Response:

Q5. Since Caroline runs a local bakery, she believes she does not need a website or social media accounts to create an online presence. Do you think she's right?

Response:

Multiple-Choice Questions:

Test your knowledge with these fun multiple-choice questions:

Q1. What is accounting?

a) The process of managing employee payroll
b) The practice of writing compelling business proposals
c) The art of marketing products and services
d) The method of recording, summarizing, and analyzing financial transactions

Q2. Why is accounting important for business owners?

a) It helps them to create killer marketing campaigns.
b) It enables them to measure their financial performance and make informed decisions.
c) It ensures that businesses always comply with environmental regulations.
d) It helps to prevent cyber attacks.

Q3. What affects how you file your taxes, shoulder liability, and deal with bankruptcy?

a) The way you write business plans and financial statements
b) The products and services you sell to your customers
c) The business model you adopt and follow
d) The stakeholders and investors you work with

Q4. What is the role of accounting in a business?

a) Designing advertising and marketing strategies
b) Managing employee performance
c) Selling products door to door
d) Analyzing financial data and preparing reports

Q5. John runs a small fast-food restaurant in his hometown. Based on this information, _____ would be the perfect business structure for him.

a) LLC
b) Sole Proprietorship

Multiple-Choice

Q1. d

Q2. b

Q3. c

Q4. d

Q5. d

True/False

Q1. False

Q2. False

Q3. False

Q4. False

Q5. True

Tips

*Be sure to check the laws and regulations in your own country to ensure compliance with state and federal authorities.

*Use online resources and contact companies such as *MyCompanyWorks.com* and *GovDocFiling.com* in the US to streamline the paperwork process and ongoing compliance requirements for your business.

* Partner with a tax specialist advisor to find the perfect business structure for your needs.

Five Cool Facts about Accounting

Before we whip into the next chapter, let's take a short break and learn some interesting facts about the wondrous world of accounting.[5][6] Here are five things about accounting we're confident you've never heard before.

The First Bookkeepers Were in Ancient Mesopotamia

It's true; accounting is as old as civilization itself!

The history of accounting can be traced to Ancient Mesopotamia, where accountants would track the taxes on sheep and farm produce.

Most Accounting Terms Have Latin Roots

Here's another fact to blow your mind: Many well-known accounting terms have Latin roots. For instance, the word 'debit' in Latin means 'he owes,' and 'accountant' comes from 'computare,' which means 'number.'

Mathematician Luca Pacioli Developed the World of Accounting

Famous Italian mathematician Luca Pacioli was the first to introduce the concept of double-entry accounting. As he liked to say, 'A person should not sleep at night until his debits equal the credits.'

Accountants Invented Bubble Gum

Here's a fun fact about accounting: A 23-year-old accountant named Water E. Diemer is the inventor of bubble gum! The inventor accidentally created bubble gum while testing recipes in 1928, saying that pink food coloring was the only thing available.

Many Oscar-Winning Films Had Accountants as Main Characters

Think Gene Wilder in *The Producers*, Charles Martin Smith in *The Untouchables*, and Ben Kingsley in *Schindler's List*. We could go on, but then this book would be a collection of Oscar-winning films!

Now that you've learned how to create the financial batter and tested your skills through our exercises, it's time we head on to the next chapter.

In Chapter Two, Caroline will discover the meaning and concepts behind commonly used accounting terms. So grab your rolling pin as we get ready to 'flourish' in the baking world and discover the fundamental concepts behind accounting. Get yourself a cupcake as we get ready to learn the sweet science of accounting in the chapters that follow!

CHAPTER 2

Mastering the Financial Landscape: Exploring Accounting Terminology and Concepts

Picture this: You're attending a seminar led by experienced professionals eager to empower you with the knowledge needed to navigate the language of money. They teach you about a fascinating realm of accounting terminology and concepts, providing a solid foundation to conquer the financial landscape.

Accounting basics will become your trusted ally as you learn to unravel the mysteries hidden within financial statements. Through practical exercises, relatable examples, and invaluable tips, you will strengthen your financial prowess and gain the skills necessary to make informed decisions that shape your financial destiny.

Imagine yourself confidently analyzing business performance, effortlessly interpreting key financial metrics, and understanding the impact of your choices on your business's financial health. With each exercise, you will sharpen your skills and develop a keen eye for financial opportunities and challenges.

So embrace the chance to delve into the depths of accounting terminology and concepts. With each page you turn, you will unlock a world of financial knowledge and embark on a transformative journey. You have the power to master the language of money, and the rewards are waiting for you. Get ready to unlock your financial potential because you will emerge from this chapter as a fluent speaker of the language of money.

Caroline's Seminar Journey: The Marvels of Accounting Unveiled

Hold tight as we embark on a thrilling adventure into the captivating realm of accounting. Whether you're a seasoned financial professional or just beginning your exploration of the accounting world, this seminar promises to provide valuable insights, practical knowledge, and a touch of wit.

So, tie on your apron and join Caroline as she attends an engaging accounting seminar and gains a treasure trove of knowledge:

Seminar Introduction:

Caroline arrives at the seminar venue, brimming with curiosity and anticipation. Fellow accounting enthusiasts greet her and receive a warm welcome from the seminar organizers. The seminar kicks off with an engaging introduction, emphasizing the vital role accounting plays in the business world and teasing the exciting topics that lie ahead.

The Language of Numbers:

In the first session, Caroline delves into the fascinating language of numbers that accounting speaks. She learns how financial information is recorded, analyzed, and communicated through various financial statements. The seminar presenter spices up the discussion with a witty remark: "Accounting is like a secret code that unlocks the story behind the numbers. Think of yourself as a financial detective with fewer trench coats and more calculators."

Mastering Financial Statements:
Caroline attends a session focused on mastering financial statements. She learns to decipher balance sheets, income statements, and cash flow statements, unraveling their hidden stories. The seminar presenter playfully quips, "Financial statements are like the magic mirrors of business. Look into them, and you'll uncover a company's financial soul. Just make sure you don't accidentally step into Narnia."

The Art of Bookkeeping:
During this session, Caroline dives into the art of bookkeeping. She learns the importance of accurate and organized record-keeping, mastering the debits and credits dance. The seminar presenter lightens the mood, saying, "Bookkeeping is like a dance routine. Debits and credits twirl around the financial stage, and your job is to ensure they never step on each other's toes. A graceful balance sheet is the grand finale."

Financial Analysis and Decision-Making:
Caroline attends a session dedicated to financial analysis and decision-making. She learns how to interpret financial ratios, evaluate company performance, and make informed business decisions based on economic data. The seminar presenter injects humor into the discussion, remarking, "Numbers might seem cold and heartless, but they hold the key to making smart business choices. Think of them as your financial fortune tellers, predicting success or warning of potential pitfalls."

Tax Tales and Adventures:
In this session, Caroline explores the captivating world of taxes. She learns about the intricacies of tax laws, deductions,

and credits and discovers strategies for optimizing tax efficiency. The seminar presenter adds a touch of wit, jokingly stating, "Taxes are like puzzles. The more deductions you find, the more money you save. But remember, unlike puzzles, the pieces of the tax code keep changing and expanding like a complex labyrinth, where new twists and turns emerge at every corner, making it an exciting challenge to find your way out!

Auditing Adventures:
Caroline dives into the thrilling world of auditing during this session. She learns about the importance of independent audits, the role of auditors, and the process of verifying financial statements. The seminar presenter lightens the mood with a humorous comment: "Auditors are the superheroes of the financial world, protecting the innocent balance sheets from the villains of financial misstatements. Capes and Spandex not included."

Ethical Challenges in Accounting:
Caroline joins a thought-provoking session on ethical challenges in accounting. She learns about the ethical responsibilities of accountants, the importance of integrity, and the impact of ethical decisions on the profession. The seminar presenter cleverly quips, "Remember, when faced with ethical dilemmas, always ask yourself, 'What would Batman do?' Well, maybe not exactly, but you get the idea."

Interactive Workshops and Networking:
Caroline participates in interactive workshops and networking opportunities with fellow participants and industry professionals throughout the seminar. These workshops provide hands-on activities, case studies, and real-world scenarios to enhance learning and practical application of accounting concepts. The seminar presenter

jokingly encourages networking, saying, "Accountants of the world, unite! Let's prove that we can be social, too, as long as it's balanced with our love for spreadsheets."

As Caroline's seminar journey concludes, she reflects on the invaluable knowledge and practical insights she has gained. Inspired and empowered, she is ready to apply her learning to her personal and professional accounting endeavors.

Remember, seizing opportunities to attend seminars and conferences allows you to expand your knowledge, network with industry experts, and stay updated on the exciting world of accounting. Embrace the adventure and continue learning in the fantastic realm of numbers and spreadsheets!

As Caroline steps out of the seminar, she realizes that now is the perfect time to review her notes. With her notebook and laptop in front of her, Caroline is ready to dough-minate the accounting world!

Now that she's stepping deeper into the world of accounting, she's about to learn new concepts and terms and why exactly she *needs* to know all of this.

A Beginner's Guide to Accounting Concepts and Terminology

Accounting is the *language* of business. It is the recording, analyzing, interpreting, and communicating financial information about an organization.

Since Caroline is still learning to master the craft of accounting, she might struggle to create relevant financial data. The result? She could lose a potential stakeholder, and that means bye-bye to expensive ingredients and never seeing her award-winning, mouth-watering cakes and brownies again.

Key Accounting Concepts: What to Know Before Getting Started

You wouldn't start baking a cake with half of the ingredients, right? In the same vein, you shouldn't establish a business without any knowledge and hope it works itself out.

What you need is a solid foundation in accounting. Here's all that Caroline picked up from her seminar:

Accrual Accounting

Accrual accounting is a lot like baking. Just as you carefully measure and combine different ingredients to create a yummy-licious cupcake, accrual accounting recognizes revenue when you *mix* and earn them rather than when the payment is made.

Take, for example, Caroline's famous 'Saturday-special' lemon meringue pie. Once she takes the sweet-smelling treat out of the oven, she puts it in the display box and considers it "ready for sale." In the same way, in accrual accounting, she would recognize her revenue when she "sells" the treat regardless of when the customers pay.

By noting expenses and revenue when they are added to the batter, Caroline can depict a more accurate picture of her company's financial performance and position. In addition, tracking financial activities more effectively allows Caroline to cut expenses.

But here's what troubles most small business owners: Is accrual or cash accounting better? Accrual accounting involves measuring and mixing all financial ingredients regardless of whether you've paid for them, whereas cash accounting is similar to baking a cake with *only* the ingredients you've paid for or received payments for.

In the former method, Caroline can enjoy recognizing transactions when they occur, just like how every ingredient contributes to the final texture and flavor of the cake, while in the latter, the focus is on cash flow, similar to how she only makes a batter with the ingredients that are readily available. The choice between the two is pretty straightforward: Large businesses (like Caroline's rival) usually prefer accrual accounting to ensure a more precise and accurate financial position, whereas small and upcoming ones (like Caroline herself) often prefer to use cash accounting. However, as she keeps inventory on hand (such as ingredients), she needs to use the accrual basis.

Going Concern

Going concern in accounting is the flour, egg, and butter of your business. Just as you assume your recipe will succeed with these foundational ingredients, going concern assumes a company will continue operating indefinitely. So when preparing financial statements, going concern helps create a rising financial picture, just like well-kneaded dough, meaning Caroline can present her bakery's assets, liabilities, revenues, and expenses based on the belief that it will continue to provide perfectly baked goods in the foreseeable future.

The benefit of this concept is that just as Caroline decorates her cake with precision, financial statements based on going concern provide a clear and accurate understanding of her bakery's financial performance. That way, she can continue making smart business decisions about viability and prospects, all the while satisfying her customers' sweet tooth.

Materiality

In accounting, materiality is like determining the minimum amount of flour, eggs, milk, sugar, and butter required to create a delicious cake.

If Caroline accidentally adds an extra pinch of sugar, her cake will still turn out perfectly flavorful; however, if she mixes too much flour and forgets the butter, her cake will taste dry and tough. Therefore, the pinch of sugar is immaterial, while the flour and butter are material because they have a substantial effect on the cake's taste and quality.

Similarly, materiality allows Caroline to identify and report information that impacts her financial statements, performance, and prospects. While minor errors and omissions won't impact her assessments, larger omissions can influence decisions considered material.

However, keep in mind that flavors are subjective to everyone's taste buds, so materiality can also vary depending on your specific circumstances.

Consistency

Running a successful bakery requires the consistency of a perfectly baked soufflé. If you add too much flour or switch butter with margarine, your soufflé will lose its fluffy texture and delicious taste.

So instead of trying to change the ingredients, it's best for Caroline to follow the same accounting methods and principles. Not only does consistency help her create mouthwatering treats, it also allows her to compare financial statements from one period to another.

As a result, she can continue improving her business while her stakeholders identify trends. Moreover, she can reduce confusion and maintain uniformity to demonstrate the reliability and integrity of her financial statements to continue rolling in the dough!

Prudence (Conservatism)

Before Caroline starts a new batch of cookies, she needs to estimate how many cookies her recipe will yield. Just like an inaccurate estimation would cost her sales, prudence allows her to be cautious when assuming yield to avoid overstating expected outcomes.

While Caroline knows her recipe can produce 24 cookies, in prudence, she assumes that she will get 20 cookies to account for the possibility of the cookies turning out larger than she expected. Similarly, prudence encourages her to be conservative in her estimates, allowing her to anticipate potential losses, liabilities, and risks.

By being cautious, Caroline can end up with a financial statement that offers a realistic and reliable depiction of her bakery. Worst case scenario? Caroline has more cookies than she imagined, and her business performs much better than expected!

Business Entity

Before Caroline starts her latest baking venture, she needs to separate ingredients and utensils for baking the cake. In the same vein, the business entity principle emphasizes the importance of treating a business separately from the owner(s). Similar to how you would likely not mix the batter of a spice cake with a rainbow confetti one, you should never merge your business and personal transactions.

Therefore, by following the business entity principle, Caroline can establish clear (and necessary) boundaries between her personal and business finances. This involves maintaining a separate bank account, tracking business expenses, and ensuring that no business funds end up mingled with personal assets.

By implementing this strategy, Caroline can create the perfect business structure and use efficient financial recipes.

With her well-prepared business entity, Caroline can create value, generate profits, and determine financial growth via income, balance, and cash flow statements (we'll learn more about this in the next chapters).

Monetary Unit Assumption

The monetary unit assumption or unity of measure assumption encourages financial transactions to be recorded in a stable currency. Take, for example, Caroline's bake sale held last week, where she sold a diverse variety of mouthwatering pies and cupcakes.

Each treat had a specific price attached to it, such as an Oreo cupcake for $5 and an apple pie slice for $4. The assumption of monetary value allows Caroline to assign a monetary value to each of her delicious treats being sold. As a result, she could record and report her bake sales and use this information to determine her total revenue.

Looking at the bigger picture, monetary unit assumption allows Caroline to create meaningful financial statements, record events in common monetary units, and ensure accurate measurement reporting. That way, she can analyze her bakery's (and her treats') financial position *and* performance.

Matching Principle

The matching principle is essential for ensuring that the expenses of baking the cupcakes are aligned with the revenue they helped generate from selling them. In simpler words, the costs incurred in producing the cupcakes should be recognized in the same accounting period as the revenue generated from selling the cupcakes.

Therefore, by matching her expenses and revenue in a particular period, Caroline can accurately assess the profitability of her bakery. If her revenue exceeds her expenses, she will enjoy a positive net income, indicating that she makes a profit. But if her expenses exceed her revenue, she will have a negative income, indicating a loss.

Revenue Recognition

Revenue recognition is just like creating a new recipe; it determines when and how to recognize and record the sweet final product (or in financial terms, revenue).

Take, for example, Caroline's monthly financial statements. When we apply the revenue recognition principle, Caroline would recognize the revenue only when the order is *delivered* to the customer. So no matter if her customers pay in advance, Caroline would only 'recognize' the revenue when the delicious cupcakes are physically transferred to the customer.

Full-Disclosure

Just like you wouldn't bake a cake without first knowing the quality of the ingredients, businesses are required to provide information like financial statements and transactions to stakeholders, investors, and creditors.

For instance, when Caroline creates her financial statements, she will have to disclose her revenue sources, expenses, liabilities, assets, and third-party transactions. Missing even one ingredient can destroy her financial batter, costing her investors and hurting her future opportunities.

Period Concept

Every time Caroline tries out a new recipe, she analyzes how much customers love it to decide whether to continue. By tracking its financial performance alongside the expenses incurred in producing it, Caroline can easily calculate its profitability.

In the sphere of accounting, this concept is referred to as period assumption. By applying this concept, Caroline can quickly identify which products attract the most buyers, the total production costs of varying treats, and total profitability during a pre-specified period.

Furthermore, the period concept allows Caroline to compare her cookie sales in July with that in June. That way, she can identify patterns, track success, and make confident business decisions to ensure her financial forecasts are as reliable as a tried-and-true recipe!

Accounting Standards

No baker trusts products with vague packaging and nonsensical designs. Instead, you look for trustworthy brands, certifications, and assurance tags. In the same vein, investors and creditors seek business owners who comply with accounting standards, including international financial reporting standards (IFRS) and generally accepted accounting principles (GAAP).

Generally, the IFRS is issued by the IASB (International Standards Board) and used across the EU, Australia, Canada, and several Asian and African countries. On the other hand, GAAP is issued by the FASB (Financial Accounting Standards Board) in the US. FASB also issues financial accounting standards (FAS) and accounting standard updates (ASU) that set or amend GAAP rules on various issues.

By following accounting standards, Caroline can ensure consistency and comparability when creating financial statements and improving reliability, transparency, and usefulness. In addition, it acts as the icing on the cake, adding a layer of credibility and trust to your financial pie.

Common Accounting Terminology

You can't run a bakery without knowing what goes into a chocolate cake, right? In a similar fashion, you can't analyze financial ingredients without knowing the right terminologies. But dough-not worry!

We're going to embark on a culinary adventure to cook up a recipe for financial success:

Accounts Payable

The thing about baking: it's expensive!

As a small business, Caroline almost always finds herself with unpaid bills for flour, sugar, and baking trays. The amount she owes to her suppliers and vendors is referred to as accounts payable.

Just like the lack of flour can affect the texture and deliciousness of her cakes, accounts payable represent the bakery's liabilities.

Accounts Receivable

Similar to us standing in front of the oven waiting for it to cook our favorite brownies, accounts receivable is the sweet anticipation of payment for treats already sold.

In simpler terms, accounts receivable is the amount owed to Caroline by her customers who paid using credit for their favorite treats. Unlike accounts payable, these represent an asset.

Equity

If Caroline bakes a cake, you wouldn't say it's yours; it belongs to the bakery until it is sold. The same is true for equity, which represents your ownership interest in a company.

More specifically, it represents the residual interest after deducting liabilities, i.e., the flour you borrowed from your neighbor.

Expenses

Making delightful cupcakes means paying for supplies, tools, and other items like administrative salaries, rent, and utilities. The total expenses incurred are referred to as the expenses of running and operating a business.

Fixed Assets

You don't chuck out your baking pans, mixers, and ovens after baking a cake, nor would you relocate to a new building for every new batch of cookies. The equipment, property, and furniture are Caroline's long-term tangible assets (or fixed assets).

Caroline will likely use fixed assets like buildings, land, and equipment for over a year for her baking endeavors.

Income Statement

The income statement is Caroline's complete record of her sales, expenses, and profit or loss. To ensure success, her income statements need to match her treats: yummy and making money!

Intangible Assets

Intangible assets are to businesses what secret recipes are to Caroline's bakery. While the top-secret recipe isn't a physical object, it holds significant value and provides Caroline a competitive advantage over other local bakeries in her town.

In the same manner, Caroline's cupcakes' reputation, customer relationships, recipes, designs, and even patents are intangible assets that contribute to the business's revenue and success!

Journal Entry

Journal entries are to business owners what recipe cards are to bakers. Each ingredient listed in a recipe is a transaction and affects the overall financial mix.

Just like you combine all the ingredients in a mixing bowl, you gather your financial transactions in a journal. Once you've mixed all the ingredients, the batter is ready to be baked.

Ledger

A ledger is to your company what a recipe book is to a chef. A recipe book allows you to note the perfect ingredients and measurements for your baking repertoire, while a ledger serves as a record book or system for documenting financial information.

With a robust ledger, Caroline can organize and keep track of her transactions.

Liabilities

Remember that time you had to race across the street for a bag of sugar but didn't have the money to pay for it? The amount you owe to the friendly shopkeeper is your "liability."

Liabilities include all the debts Caroline owes to third parties, like loans and accrued expenses.

Liquidity

Liquidity is Caroline's ability to meet her short-term obligations and convert assets into cash quickly. While the most obvious liquid asset is the cash lying in Caroline's register, liquidity can also include inventory and accounts receivable.

For Caroline, liquidity is the ability to have enough cash to pay for that flour and sugar.

Net Income
Net income is the first look at your delicious-smelling, fluffy cake pulled right out of the oven. It's the delightful and sweet outcome of all of Caroline's baking efforts, minus the cost of the ingredients and taxes. It is the sign of the company's profitability.

Prepaid Expenses
Before Caroline starts baking mouth-watering cupcakes, she needs a rental space, insurance, and supplies. Since Caroline pays for several months of rent upfront and uses the space over time, these costs are considered 'prepaid expenses.'

Revenue
Revenue is the icing on top of the perfect birthday cake. It represents her company's sales that make her baking dreams *rise* to the top!

Solvency
Different than liquidity, solvency is Caroline's ability to meet long-term obligations and continue operations in the near future. For instance, if she decides to invest in her dream oven and refrigeration units, solvency would involve ensuring she has enough funds to support their long-term operations.

Trial Balance
Before introducing a new flavor of cupcake to her customers, Caroline tests and tries the goods herself. In the same

manner, the trial balance represents an intermediate step used to detect potential errors and imbalances.

When creating her trial balance, Caroline would have to include all revenue, expense, asset, and liability accounts. Yep, it's an important step!

Valuation
Just like Caroline likes to start every new month by assessing the value of the flour, sugar, oil, butter, etc., that she has on hand and the product she's already made, valuation encourages business owners to determine the monetary value of *all* business assets.

Here's the best part: Valuation is not limited to physical products. So Caroline can evaluate the worth of her equipment, assets, bakery, and the brand itself.

Working Capital
Working capital is similar to the difference between a collection of ingredients in Caroline's pantry and the ones she's borrowed from her next-door neighbor. In simpler words, it represents the available operational liquidity.

So as Caroline strives to create the perfect balance between eggs and flour, she also has to maintain a balanced mixture of current assets and liabilities. If not, her business might sink like bread with too little yeast.

The Importance of Accounting Concepts and Terminology
Accounting concepts and terminology serve as the building blocks for understanding financial information. Without grasping these terms and concepts, your ability to interpret financial statements will collapse, just like a cake with too much butter.

baking stages, the segregation of duties in financial processes ensures that every individual is responsible for a different task. That way, no single person has to bear the burden of processing all transactions or has complete control over financial transactions.

- **Owner Approval of Transactions-** Like no employee would introduce a new recipe in Caroline's bakery without first consulting her, internal accounting policies require organizations to get the owner's approval to ensure each financial activity is sanctioned and approved by the business owner.

- **Counter Representatives-** Just like the Sweet Caroline Bakery can't run without a cashier to handle cash, keep receipts, and maintain orders, you need someone to organize your financial information. This way, you can ensure a clear financial record, making it easy to keep track of your revenue and expenses.

- **Hiring a Bookkeeper-** Whenever Caroline creates a new recipe, she stores it in her recipe book to ensure she always has a record of her yummylicious recipes. In the same vein, bookkeepers are record-keepers, recording financial transactions in accounting software, preparing bank reconciliation, and doing all of the tricky financial-related tasks.

- **Outsourcing an Accountant-** Just like Caroline's master pastry chef brings unique expertise to the table, outsourcing a professional accountant allows her to tap into unmatched knowledge. With the help of a proficient accountant, Caroline can ease the financial statement preparation and reviewing process and access insightful guidance.

- **Daily Bank Deposits-** Business owners should deposit their cash into the bank daily to minimize on-site cash accumulation and the risk of theft.

- **Scan All Your Invoices and Receipts-** Similar to how Caroline keeps copies of her recipes on her computer to avoid losing them, business owners need to digitize invoices and receipts to ensure an electronic record of transactions, making it easier to track and retrieve information.
- **Monitoring and Reporting Concerns-**Caroline conducts multiple taste and quality checks during baking to ensure that her baked treats are up to her standards. Similarly, business owners must encourage employees to audit financial records and transactions and report concerns to authorities to catch illicit activities.
- **Risk Mitigation-** When trying a new recipe, Caroline follows it with precision to avoid destroying its taste or look. To mitigate the risk of getting into financial trouble, Caroline must identify the potential risks in her accounting system.

Building Blocks of Financial Understanding: Accounting Basics

When baking, Caroline meticulously measures the amount of ingredients to pour into her batter. After that, she picks the perfect baking tray and sets the oven timer to just the right number of minutes to ensure perfection.

It's when all the pieces of the recipe come together that Caroline can bake award winning bread. The same is true for accounting, where you need to understand the building blocks of the financial mixture before you can reap the rewards of your efforts.

So let's dive into the world of record-keeping and how to ensure financial perfection.

Classifying Accounts: Sorting out the Pieces

Accounts, in accounting, are as important as the baking ingredients lining Caroline's pantry. Imagine if she picked salt instead of sugar; her whole cake would be ruined!

Similarly, as we discussed earlier, knowing the right accounts to add into your mix is crucial for baking success:

- **Assets:** These are the valuable ingredients required in the baking process and are owned by Caroline.
- **Liabilities:** These represent all the flour, sugar, and baking trays that you borrowed or bought on credit.
- **Equity:** Equity reflects the assets that are left after deducting liabilities.
- **Revenue:** Revenue is the income from primary business activities.
- **Expenses:** These are the costs of doing business, including supplies, rent, and salaries.

Recording Transactions: Completing the Puzzle Pieces

Transactions are the essential ingredients of your financial recipes. By recording transactions at the right time, you can create a clear picture of your company's financial activities.

That's where journal entries come in. Before Caroline starts creating her journal entries, she'll have to be familiar with the following common business transactions:

- **Sales:** When Caroline sells her products, she records it as a credit to the sales account and a debit to cash or accounts receivable. The total baked goods sold represent her bakery's total revenue.
- **Purchases:** On the other hand, when Caroline goes shopping for butter, eggs, and new and exciting baking pans, she records it as a debit to the inventory or

supplies account and a credit to cash or accounts payable.

- **Receipts:** Every time a new customer pops in to try Caroline's famous cupcakes, she creates a record of the payment received from the customer, i.e., credit to a sales account and debit to cash or accounts receivables.

- **Employee Compensation:** As Caroline's popularity grows, she needs to hire new employees. Now she needs to record a debit to payroll expenses and a credit to cash and payroll liabilities.

The Accounting Cycle: Completing the Puzzle Again and Again

https://www.accountrely.com/single-post/2018/03/19/an-introduction-to-the-accounting-cycle

The accounting cycle is like a never-ending puzzle. Accountants follow a seemingly endless series of steps to create accurate financial reports. But luckily for you, we're going to learn how to do this the easy way (less steps but equally effective!).

Here's a simplified version of the accounting cycle:

1. **Recording Transactions:** Each transaction is recorded in a physical or digital journal and acts as the initial puzzle piece. Here's how this step works:

   Choose a Journal- She needs to decide on the type of journal she will use to record her details.

   Record the Details- Once she finds the perfect journal, Caroline can start recording the date, description, and accounts of each transaction.

2. **Posting to General Ledger:** The puzzle pieces are transferred to the general ledger, where accounts are updated with transaction details.

   The general ledger acts as an oven, combining everything to allow you to create financial success. Here are the steps:

   Setting up the General Ledger- Caroline needs to create a general ledger with separate accounts for every asset, liability, revenue, expense, and equity. We've covered this step in Chapter 1.

   Transfer Information- The transaction information recorded in the journals will be transferred to the respective general ledger accounts.

3. **Trial Balance:** A trial balance is prepared to ensure the debits and credits balance. Here's a step-by-step guide:

   List All Accounts- Trial balances showcase a business's accounts from a general ledger.

Calculate Totals- The next step is to calculate the total of the debit and credit balances. Lastly, she has to verify these to ensure the financial records are in balance.

4. **Adjusting Entries:** Adjustments are made to reflect deferrals and accruals accurately. Just like Caroline might adjust her cake recipe to enhance the flavor and texture of the cake, small businesses might tweak their entries to reflect deferrals and accruals.

   Here's how this works:

   Update Account Balances- After she adjusts her financial recipe, Caroline must update account balances in the general ledger. These entries act as new recipes, allowing Caroline to adjust them based on what's missing.

   Finally Making the Entries- Once Caroline knows what she needs to adjust, she can start making her adjusting entries. Now she can start creating the final version of her financial records.

5. **Adjusted Trial Balance:** An adjusted trial balance is prepared to verify the accuracy of the accounts after adjustments. Finally, after adjusting her entries and trial balance, Caroline can ensure that her financial records are fully updated.

6. **Financial Statements:** Financial statements are prepared to present the complete financial picture using the adjusted trial balance. (Don't worry, you'll learn all about the wondrous world of financial statements in the next chapter.)

Preparing financial statements is like decorating the cake to make it more appealing. With these, you can unlock an in-depth view of your business's financial performance, cash flow, and position.

7. **Closing Entries:** Temporary accounts are closed to start fresh for the next accounting period.

8. **Post-closing Trial Balance:** The balance ensures that all temporary accounts are closed, leaving only permanent accounts. Just like Caroline cleans the kitchen after a day of hard work, you can close your temporary accounts to start the new cycle.

The accounting cycle repeats with each new accounting period, allowing businesses to track and report their financial activities continuously. While writing and tracking every little financial activity would leave Caroline with no time to bake or sell her products, software and automation tools make it easy.

With the help of the right accounting software, you can create well-written and easy-to-digest financial statements. But for this, you'll have to wait a few chapters!

Reporting: Piecing Together the Puzzle
Once all the puzzle pieces are in place, it's time to unveil the complete picture through financial reporting. Financial statements serve as the key output of this process, providing stakeholders with valuable insights into a company's financial performance and position. Let's explore the main financial statements (look for more on this in the next chapter):

Income Statement:
This statement summarizes a company's revenues and deducts all expenses incurred during a specific period. It shows whether the company made a profit or incurred a loss.

Balance Sheet:
The balance sheet provides a snapshot of a company's financial position at a given time. It showcases the company's assets, liabilities, and equity, allowing stakeholders to assess its financial health.

Statement of Cash Flow:
This statement records the cash inflow and outflow during a specific period. It categorizes cash flow into multiple activities, including operating, financing, and investing to provide insights into a company's liquidity and cash management.

Now that we've covered the basics of accounting, it's time to test our skills! Let's check out some exercises and examples to solidify our newly learned knowledge.

Test Your Knowledge: Fun Exercises, Examples, and Tips
Questions

Q1. Caroline is still new to the world of financial accounting. In your words, explain how you think her newfound knowledge of accounting terminologies and concepts benefits her.

Response:

Q2. Caroline also learned about accrual and deferral. Unfortunately, she found the two terminologies confusing. Explain the similarities and differences between the two (try to use an example).

Response:

Short Questions

Answer the following questions in two to three sentences.

Q1. Explain depreciation in accounting.

Response:

Q2. What is the difference between accounts payable and accounts receivable?

Response:

Q3. What is the difference between debit and credit in accounting?

Response:

Q4. Explain what the matching principle is and its importance.

Response:

Q5. Differentiate between assets and liabilities. Try using a vivid example:

Response:

Multiple-Choice Questions

Q1. Which financial statement provides an overview of a business's financial position at a specific time?

a) Income statement
b) Cash flow statement
c) Balance sheet
d) Retained earnings statement

Q2. The listing of all of the available accounts for use in a company's accounting system is called:

a) Debit
b) Chart of accounts
c) Credit
d) Cash flow

Q3. Which of the following is not a core financial statement?

a) Balance sheet
b) Cash flow statement
c) Trial balance
d) Income statement

Q4. Under accrual accounting, revenues are reported when which of the following occurs?

a) Cash is received
b) Goods have been delivered
c) Earnings are retained
d) None of these

Q5. When are liabilities recorded under accrual basis accounting?

    a) When incurred
    b) At the end of the fiscal year
    c) When paid
    d) Whenever the business owner wants

True/False

Now mark true and false to test your knowledge:

Q1. Accrual accounting recognizes revenue when you receive or pay cash.

        True   False

Q2. Long-term liabilities represent financial obligations that are due within a year.

        True   False

Q3. The matching principle in accounting requires expenses to match revenues in a particular period.

        True   False

Q4. Prepaid expenses are assets that represent future expenses paid in advance.

        True   False

Q5. Accounts payable represents the money owed to a business from its suppliers for goods/services purchased on credit.

        True   False

Answers:

Q1. Learning accounting terminologies and concepts offers numerous benefits to Caroline. With her newfound knowledge, she can make informed financial decisions by learning about financial statements, cash flow management, monitor business performance, and unlock financing and investment opportunities.

Q2. Accrual and deferral are similar in the sense that they both relate to the recognition of revenue and expenses. The primary difference between the two principles is the timing of when these transactions are recorded in financial statements. While accrual recognizes income when it is earned and expenses when they are incurred, deferral 'defers' the recognition until the goods are physically transferred.

For example, if Caroline delivers a large order of custom-made cakes for an event in January and sends the invoice in February, in accrual, she would recognize the revenue in January, regardless of the timing of the cash receipt. Therefore, Caroline would recognize the revenue made from her custom-made cakes in January, despite the fact that she invoices the customer in February.

On the contrary, in deferral accounting, if a customer pays in advance for a large wedding order in January and the order is for a February event, Caroline would recognize this as deferred revenue in January. Instead, she would not recognize the actual revenue until the order had been delivered in February.

Short Questions

Q1. Depreciation is the allocation of the cost of a long-term asset over its useful life to reflect the gradual loss in its value.

Q2. Accounts payable refers to the money owed by a company to third-party suppliers, vendors, and stakeholders. On the contrary, accounts receivable is the money owed to a company by its customers and clients.

Q3. Debits are entries made on the left side of an account that increase assets and decreases liabilities and equity, whereas credits are entries on the right side that decrease assets and increases liabilities and equity.

Q4. The matching principle is an accounting principle that allows accountants to recognize expenses in the same period as the related revenue. The principle is essential because it reflects the profitability of a business by aligning the time of revenue and expenses. It also helps create reliable financial statements and provides accurate reflections of financial performance.

Q5. Assets represent the resources owned by a company boasting economic value, whereas liabilities are the company's obligations and debt that it needs to pay. For instance, the refrigeration units in Caroline's bakery are her assets, while the loan she takes from the bank represents her liabilities.

Multiple-Choice

Q1. c

Q2. b

Q3. c

Q4. b

Q5. a

True/False

Q1. False

Q2. False

Q3. True

Q4. True

Q5. False

Tips

* Handle your paperwork on a daily or weekly basis so it does not build up.
* Reconcile your bank account monthly to spot anomalies.
* Use accounting software that matches your business needs.

Congratulations! You've completed another chapter; here's a slice of cake to help you celebrate. Done? Now let's get started with the next chapter; it's time we unravel financial statements and their ins and outs.

CHAPTER 3

Exploring the Financial Sphere: What a Financial Statement Means and Why It Matters

You've probably heard the saying you can't improve what you can't *see*. When it comes to running a business, nothing could be truer than this adage. But without financial statements, i.e., the secret ingredient to success, you might struggle to identify your business's expenses, profits, and losses.

On the contrary, diving deep into financial statements provides you with insightful information on income and changes in equity, determines financial challenges, helps you to enjoy a competitive edge, and creates the perfect mix for business success.

The bad news: you can't write half-decent financial statements without *at least* a basic understanding of accounting. The good news: Caroline is just about at the right place in her journey to learn how to create, read, and understand financial statements as thoroughly as she understands the art of making cookies!

So don your apron and roll up your sleeves; it's time to bake up a financial storm! In this chapter, you and Caroline will learn how to crunch the numbers to create and understand a killer financial statement:

The First Look: What Are Financial Statements Anyway?

Before you preheat your oven and get started, it's essential to take a step back and understand what financial statements *mean*. Put simply, they are a picture of the past in order to determine how to move into the future.

Financial statements represent a business's financial activity and performance, including insights into a company's cash flow.

Every baking adventure starts with picking the essential ingredients, and the same is true for your financial statements. You'll need the following three types of financial statements to get accurate numbers:

- Balance Sheet
- Income Statement
- Cash Flow Statement

The Need for Financial Statements: Why They Matter for Your Business

Financial statements are your *recipe* for success. But like everyone's favorite rainbow cake, financial statements have layers.

There are endless benefits of creating—or learning how to write—a financial statement, including:

Enhancing Your Budget Allocation

If you're a small business, increasing revenue is likely at the top of your wish list. Fortunately, Caroline doesn't need a measuring cup to analyze how well she's hitting her goals.

All she needs is a well-written and detailed financial statement to determine which goods sell the best and attract the most customers. That way, she can allocate her budget for sustainable growth.

Helping Cut Costs
Caroline doesn't *really* need every new kitchen gadget on the market. What she needs to do is rise to the occasion and determine the unnecessary costs sabotaging her bottom line.

A financial statement can help her learn to cut costs and discover affordable alternatives to a $100 baking tray! With a financial statement, business owners can find areas to save costs, create smart budgets, and wave goodbye to overspending.

Offering Insights into Your Financial Position
You wouldn't throw milk and butter into your batter without ensuring they're fresh. In the same way, you shouldn't make huge business decisions before first viewing where you stand financially.

Fortunately, by preparing a financial statement, Caroline can determine her company's performance at a specific time. The result? She can present her finances to stakeholders with a cup full of confidence.

Aiding in Decision-Making
If you're short on butter, you've got to improvise and throw in a little oil to create the same fluffy and soft cake texture. Similarly, when it comes to running a business, Caroline needs to grasp the different ways she can grow.

Financial statements are the yeast of your dough, activating new opportunities and helping you to expand and make smart business decisions.

Providing the Bigger Picture
You can't hit your long-term business goals if you're only focused on the next sale. To increase profitability, Caroline needs to align her financial position with her short- and long-

term goals. Only then can she enjoy the sweet results of her financial recipe.

Allowing You to Get Credit
It's no surprise that creditors and lenders don't want to invest in an over-leveraged business. By creating a financial report, Caroline can show that her financial performance, like her cupcakes, is baked to perfection.

Promoting Accurate Financial Ratios
Financial statements can identify profitability, valuation, and solvency ratios to ensure that financial performance doesn't crumble under pressure. (Psst... we'll learn more about profitability, solvency, and all the other types of ratios in the following chapters.)

Facilitating Performance Evaluation
Financial statements are useful in assessing the business's performance to find areas of improvement and manage risks to ensure financial success.

The Three Types of Financial Statements and How to Read Them
Sure, financial statements sound like a *piece of cake,* but not when you start writing and analyzing one. Before you begin panic-baking, it's simple; you only need a little guidance.

Let's learn how to create one that's baked to perfection.

Balance Sheet
Balance sheets, just like recipe cards, spell out the mix you need to create the perfect outcome. This includes the perfect combination of liabilities and equity, which add together to make up your assets.

Since Caroline is still new to the world of financial statements, a balance sheet makes *zero* sense to her. But that's all right; here we have an example with just the right ingredients to help her understand every component of a balance sheet:

Balance Sheet

All figures in USD millions unless stated	Year 1	Year 2	Year 3
Cash	7,170	5,635	4,279
Accounts Receivable	16,220	17,193	18,225
Inventories	9,124	9,671	10,251
Total Current Assets	32,514	32,499	32,755
Property Plant & Equipment	23,217	24,610	26,086
TOTAL ASSETS	55,731	57,109	58,841
Accounts Payable	12,165	12,895	13,669
Deferred Taxes	910	1,058	1,216
Total Current Liabilities:	13,075	13,952	14,884
Long-Term Debt	18,000	16,000	14,000
Common Equity	8,127	8,627	9,127
Retained Earnings	16,528	18,529	20,830
Total Shareholders' Equity	24,655	27,156	29,957
LIABILITIES & EQUITY	55,731	57,109	58,841

https://corporatefinanceinstitute.com/resources/accounting/three-financial-statements/

Did you take a good look at the balance sheet sample? We know: It's *soooo* confusing! But worry not, for we're going to dive into the different components of a balance sheet below.

Plus, you might recognize a lot of these terms from Chapter 2! (If you don't remember the exact meaning, you can take a quick look, we'll wait.)

Assets

Assets are to your business what fresh ingredients and baking essentials are to Caroline's bakery. Just as Caroline needs flour, milk, sugar, butter, and trays, a business's assets include cash and physical assets like buildings or equipment.

Think of assets as everything that adds economic value to your business, such as machinery, land inventory, trademarks, and investments. Take, for example, Caroline's new $500 multi-use mixer, bought with the expectation that it will save time and bring increased income by creating a dough-licious feast.

Just like the endless flavors of ice cream, assets can be of various types based on flexibility and usage. But let's discuss the two most important ones (no, not vanilla and chocolate): long- and short-term assets.

Short-Term Assets (Current Assets)

Short-term assets are items that are held for less than a year, like the ingredients in Caroline's pantry.

Moreover, short-term assets will be converted into cash. You can think of short-term assets as the raw ingredients, packaging materials, and prepaid expenses in Caroline's kitchen.

Long-Term Assets

Long-term assets are your refrigeration, mixers, and ovens, things that will benefit your company for over a year. These are also referred to as non-current assets and can be tangible or intangible.

Liabilities

Liabilities include obligations and debts that Caroline owes to suppliers and lenders, for example.

Once you've made magic with the ingredients you've bought on credit, you need to settle your liabilities by paying them back. Generally, liabilities are of two primary types:

Short-Term Liabilities (Current Liabilities)

Short-term liabilities are debts expected to be settled in a specified time. These include accounts payable and accrued expenses, which we discussed in earlier chapters.

Long-Term Liabilities

Long-term liabilities are financial obligations extending beyond one year. These could include tax liabilities, bonds payable, and lease or loan obligations.

Equity

Equity represents all the pieces of the cake left over once all the guests (debt) have left.

Your equity value can be positive or negative, depending on how well you're performing. If Caroline's bakery performs well and her shareholders' equity is positive, it means she's got enough cake to satisfy her own cravings. But if it's negative, that means no cake slices are left for her, and she has to wash the dishes.

Now that Caroline has learned the basic elements of a balance sheet, it's time to grab your calculators and do a little math (we promise it's not too difficult!).

The Magic Equation: Assets= Liabilities + Shareholders' Equity

If Caroline wants to knead her way to success, she's got to remember the ingredients to the magic concoction:

Liabilities + Shareholders' Equity = Assets

Now Caroline can create fantastic balance sheets, but she's only getting started. The next step is to uncover the intricacies of an income statement.

Income Statement

Now that Caroline can read her balance sheets, it's time to flip the page and move on to the next financial obstacle. Your income statement is like a layered confetti cake, each filled with new flavors and ingredients.

Take a look at this example, and let's start unraveling the key components of this complex financial statement:

Income Statement

All figures in USD millions unless stated	Year 1	Year 2	Year 3
Revenue	98,671	104,591	110,867
Cost of Goods Sold	44,402	47,066	49,890
Gross Profit	54,269	57,525	60,977
Distribution Expenses	7,400	7,844	8,315
Marketing and Administration	32,063	33,346	34,680
Research and Development	2,269	2,406	2,550
Depreciation	3,157	3,347	3,548
EBIT (Operating Profit)	9,379	10,583	11,884
Interest	1,178	1,054	930
Income Before Taxes	8,201	9,529	10,954
Total Taxes	2,460	2,859	3,286
Net Income	5,740	6,670	7,668

Revenue

Revenue is all the dough rolling in from the sale of cupcakes, pastries, and other baked goods, as well as the income Caroline generates from her baking-related services.

It represents the sweet rewards of her bakery's activities during a predefined accounting period. Moreover, revenue contributes significantly to the increase in Caroline's bakery's equity.

Cost of Goods Sold

Caroline incurred cost in buying the ingredients for her mouthwatering cupcakes. It's not like you can get the raw materials for free, right? But when calculating the cost of goods, Caroline will also have to account for packaging material, direct labor, and baking supplies.

Gross Profit

What do you get when you subtract your costs of goods sold from revenue? Gross profit and a slice of cake for your hard work!

Gross profit or margin is basically the profit Caroline earns from her monthly sales *after* costs of goods sold but *before* accounting for her many other expenses.

Expenses (Distribution, Marketing and Admin, R&D, Depreciation)

Expenses are all the costs incurred in running the bakery. When creating an income statement, expenses must be recorded to help determine profitability.

Typically, this section of the income statement includes rent, labor expenses, utilities, marketing and advertising, and maintenance or repairs. Although that sounds like a lot, the calculation is super simple.

Operating Profit

Operating profit represents the financial performance of a business's core. Just like Caroline's cake's core determines its taste, texture, and quality, operating profit reveals the profitability and success of a business's daily activities.

To calculate operating profits, Caroline needs to subtract the cost of the ingredients and supplies used for making her products (aka the cost of goods) and the expenses incurred in running her bakery (aka operating expenses) from the total revenue she generates from selling her cakes (or the net sales revenue).

Taxes

You can't do much without hearing the word *taxes*. If you shuddered just like Caroline, worry not; we'll learn what taxes are in the simplest possible way.

Income tax is applied after agreement with the relevant tax authorities, after which every cake comes with at least one less slice. The good news: Taxes are only calculated on the company's taxable income. The bad news? Taxes are calculated on *all* your taxable income.

Net Income

Your net income shows how delicious your cake *really* is. By calculating this, Caroline can identify how profitable her bakery is and whether she's incurring losses.

It's simple: If the revenue minus the cost of goods sold, expenses, and taxes is positive, you're in a sweet position. But if it's a **negative** figure, it's time to take a closer look at your business model.

Doing the Math: Learning to Calculate Net Income

We know: more math? Before you throw this book across the room, hold on a second. This equation is super easy; you won't even need to do long division.

Here's what the income statement looks like:

"Net Income = (Revenue + Gains) – (CoGS + Expenses + Losses + Taxes)"

Or in even simpler terms:

"Net Income = Total Revenue – Total Expenses"

Now that Caroline understands what all these terms mean, she can calculate her net income. Here's how she does it:

→ First, she calculates her total revenue, including the sales, fees, and income earned from other business activities.

→ After that, she calculates the cost of goods, such as raw materials, labor, and so on.

→ Next, she adds the rent, utilities, and other costs to calculate her total expenses.

→ After that, she identifies any losses or gains (no, leftovers don't count!)

→ Now she can use the formula mentioned above to determine how well her business is doing.

The Financial Duo: Income Statement and Accounting Equation

Caroline doesn't only want to bake the best cupcakes in town; she also wants to cook up a recipe for financial success. And for that, she needs to go beyond simple plus and minus and look at the bigger picture.

When you mix the income statement with the accounting equation, you have the means to really dig deeply into your financial position.

With the accounting equation, you can determine the change in equity, total assets, and liabilities, without which Caroline would be at a loss. But armed with these important numbers, she can review performance, identify trends, and forecast budgets to minimize the roadblocks holding her back from delighting even more people with her sweet cupcakes.

But wait! The financial duo is *awesome,* but it's not *everything.* By now, we've covered income statements and balance sheets, which leaves us one last crucial financial statement.

Let's explore the ins and outs of cash flow statements so you can see the whole picture.

Cash Flow Statement
Until her cash flow is as smooth as her butter cream frosting, Caroline needs to learn how it works and ways she can improve. The cash flow statement tells you where exactly your money is coming from and where it's going.

But it's not that simple. Let's not waste any more time; here's why cash flow statements can be a bit confusing and how you can easily master them.

Before you start writing your own cash flow statement, take a look at this sample:

Cash Flow Statement

All figures in USD millions unless stated	Year 1	Year 2	Year 3
CASH FROM OPERATING			
Net Income	5,740	6,670	7,668
Deferred Taxes	329	147	158
Depreciation	3,157	3,347	3,548
Cash From Working Capital Items	(1,498)	(791)	(838)
Subtotal	7,729	9,374	10,536
CASH FROM INVESTING			
Capital Expenditure	(5,199)	(4,740)	(5,024)
Subtotal	(5,199)	(4,740)	(5,024)
CASH FROM FINANCING			
Change in Long-Term Debt	(2,000)	(2,000)	(2,000)
Change in Common Equity	500	500	500
Dividends	(4,018)	(4,669)	(5,368)
Subtotal	(5,518)	(6,169)	(6,868)
CASH BALANCE			
Beginning of the Year	10,159	7,170	5,635
Increase / (Decrease)	(2,989)	(1,535)	(1,356)
End of the Year	7,170	5,635	4,279

Operating Activities

The operating activities track how much cash Caroline makes from selling her treats. In addition, it also includes how much cash she spent on buying flour, eggs, sugar, yeast, and the baking tray she promises she *needs*.

To better understand this, Caroline looks at another example:

Net Income- $500,000

Payroll- $75,000

Depreciation- $20,000

Bakery Rent- $35,000

Accounts Receivable Increase- $25,000

Grab your calculators; it's time to understand how you can calculate the total:

For this, we use the formula: "Net Income + Depreciation – Accounts Receivable Increase = Cash from Operating Activities"

In the first step, Caroline identifies her net income and depreciation. Next, she adds them to get a total figure of $520,000. She did not use the payroll or bakery rent figures as those would have already been deducted to arrive at net income.

After that, she subtracts the accounts receivable increase, i.e., $25,000, from the figure presented above.

As a result, she gets the correct net cash from operating activities, which is $495,000.

Financing Activities

If you didn't catch it from the name, financing activities include cash from, well, financing activities. Take, for example, how Caroline recently took a bank loan to expand her operation and hire drivers to deliver her treats.

This loan will appear in her financing activities alongside cash from investors and/or banks. Here's how Caroline can calculate her financing activities cash flow (heads up! It's harder than that for operating activities).

Cash flow = new loans received + equity investments + new capital leases - dividend payments

Here's a quick example:

New Debt Loans Received- $60,000

Equity Investments- $30,000

New Capital Leases- $15,000

Dividend Payments- $25,000

Once Caroline puts these values in the above-mentioned formula, she gets $80,000. Now try to calculate on your own to see if you get the same value. Thus, her cash flow from all her financing activities of the year equals $80,000.

Investing Activities
When Caroline buys a new oven for her bakery, this cost adds up in her investing activities. This section reflects all the cash flows related to changes in equipment, assets, and investments.

You ask, How do I calculate *this?* It's simple; you only need to add the purchase/sale of property/equipment with the purchase/sale of marketable securities and other businesses.

Here's a look at Caroline's recent purchases and sales to better understand investing activities:

Equipment sales- $120,000

Property purchase- $85,000

Net cash from investing- $35,000

The Concoction to Success: Balance Sheet, Income Statement, and Cash Flow Statement
You've never heard someone say only flour is essential for baking. It's when you add all the right ingredients that you

can create a delectable treat. In the same vein, you can't create a financial recipe with just one of the three main financial statements.

Each financial statement reflects different yet crucial components, such as liabilities and assets in the balance sheet, net income in the income statement, and financing costs in the cash flow statement. By linking these financial ingredients, Caroline can identify the drivers for her business and make future forecasts (more on that in Chapter 7).

Now that you're filled to the brim with knowledge of financial statements, we're sure you're buzzing to test yourself, right? Lucky for you, we've created a host of exciting questions, exercises, and examples to help you identify how many new things you've learned.

Test Your Knowledge: Fun Exercises, Examples, and Tips Questions

Q1. Create a balance sheet, income statement, and cash flow statement based on the information provided:

Balance Sheet Information:

Cash- $10,050

Accounts Receivable- $4,500

Inventory- $15,000

Equipment- $50,000

Liabilities and Shareholders' Equity:

Accounts Payable- $7,550

Long-Term Debts- $20,000

Shareholders' Equity- $52,000

Income Statement Information:

Sales Revenue- $100,000

Cost of Goods Sold- $35,000

Operating Expenses- $32,000

Interest Expenses- $2,500

Income Tax Expenses- $7,800

Cash Flow Statement Information:

Operating Activities Cash Flow- $30,200

Investing Activities Cash Flow- $205,000

Financing Activities Cash Flow- $4,000

Response:

Q2. Identify the major components of the financial statements and how they relate to other operations in accounting.

Response:

Short Questions

Answer the following short questions in two to three sentences.

Q1. What is a balance sheet, and what is its purpose?

Response:

Q2. Caroline is preparing to create her financial statements. But for this, she needs to know the formula for calculating shareholders' equity and net income. Help her recall them.

Response:

Q3. What does a cash flow statement reveal about your business?

Response:

Q4. What do "liabilities" mean on a financial statement?

Response:

Q5. Why do businesses need to present financial statements to investors and stakeholders?

Response:

Multiple-Choice Questions

Choose the right option and check the answers below to verify your answers:

Q1. _____ tells you where your money is coming from and where it is going.

    a) Income statement
    b) Balance sheet
    c) Cash flow statement
    d) Statement of retained earnings

Q2. Which of the following is **not** a benefit of a financial statement?

    a) Helps cut costs
    b) Aids in decision making
    c) Allows for better hiring decisions
    d) Promotes accurate financial ratios

Q3. The main sections on a balance sheet are:

    a) Assets, liabilities, income
    b) Assets, equity, expenses
    c) Assets, liabilities, equity
    d) Assets, gains, equity

Q4. The balance sheet equation is represented as:

a) Revenues = expenses + net income
b) Cash outflows = cash inflows - net cash flow
c) Assets = liabilities + shareholders' equity
d) Retained earnings = dividends + net income

Q5. Which of these scenarios causes an increase in accounts payable?

a) Bakery supplies are purchased with cash
b) Customers pay late invoices
c) Business owner goes shopping
d) The supplier delivers raw materials on credit

True/False

Tick the best answer using your knowledge:

Q1. The income statement reports the profitability of your business at specific times.

True   False

Q2. The cash flow statement provides payroll information for your business.

True   False

Q3. Gross Profit is equal to revenue less taxes.

True   False

Q4. A new loan is shown on the cash flow statement in financing activities.

True   False

Q5. With the income statement, you can find out your company's equity at a specific period.

True	False

Answers:

Q1. Balance Sheet

Date: [Insert Date]

Assets:

Cash- $10,050

Accounts Receivable- $4,500

Inventory- $15,000

Equipment- $50,000

Total Assets- $79,550

Liabilities and Shareholders' Equity:

Accounts Payable- $7,550

Long-Term Debts- $20,000

Shareholders' Equity- $52,000

Total Liabilities and Shareholders' Equity- $79,550

Income Statement

For the Period [Date]

Sales Revenue- $100,000

Cost of Goods Sold- $35,000

Gross Profit - $65,000

Operating Expenses- $32,000

Operating Profit - $33,000

Interest Expenses- $2,500

Income Before Taxes - $30,500

Income Tax Expenses- $7,800

Net Income- $22,700

Cash Flow Statement

For the Period [Insert Date]

Cash flow from Operating Activities- $30,200

Cash flow from Investing Activities- $205,000

Cash flow from Financing Activities- $4,000

Total Cash Flow- $239,200

Q2. The major components of a financial statement are a balance sheet, cash flow statement, and income statement. Although each statement provides different information about a company's performance and position, they are interconnected.

For starters, the balance sheet provides a snapshot of a company's liabilities, assets, and shareholders' equity, which can impact the income statement and cash flow statement. In addition, the income statement showcases net income or net loss over a specific period by calculating earnings, revenue, expenses, and taxes.

The net income from this section is transferred to the balance sheet, making them interdependent. Lastly, the cash flow statement provides in-depth information on the sources and uses of cash, which are mostly derived from the income statement.

Short Questions

Q1. Balance sheets provide a detailed view of a company's financial position at a specific point. They showcase the company's liabilities, assets, and shareholders' equity.

Q2. Shareholders' Equity = Total Assets – Total Liabilities. Net Income = Total Revenue – Total Expenses

Q3. Cash flow statements reveal how cash is generated and used by a business. It allows you to highlight cash inflows and outflows from multiple activities.

Q4. The liabilities section features the company's obligations and debts owed to third parties like loans, accounts payable, and accrued expenses.

Q5. Financial statements offer in-depth information about a company's financial performance, position, and cash flows. As a result, stakeholders can make informed decisions, and investors can determine whether the business is worth investing in.

Multiple-Choice

Q1. c

Q2. c

Q3. c

Q4. c

Q5. d

True/False

Q1. True

Q2. False

Q3. False

Q4. True

Q5. False

Tips

* Make sure you carefully review your monthly financial statements to spot areas of improvement and potential issues before they grow out of control.
* Consider reviewing your supporting reports, such as Accounts Receivable and Accounts Payable Aging Reports, with current and past due invoices from customers, vendors, and stakeholders so that you don't make or receive late payments.
* Ensure you follow a clear and consistent formatting style to avoid confusion when reviewing or comparing financial statements.

Take a rest; here's a milkshake and cookie for your hard work! Now that you've completed Chapter 3 and its challenging activities, you can produce phenomenal financial statements and grow your business.

But since there are more exciting chapters in this book, it's obvious there's still a whole lot more for you to learn before you call yourself a skilled accountant! So let's not waste any time and take you on a brand-new accounting adventure!

CHAPTER 4

Putting Your Skills to the Test: Learning to Calculate Financial Ratios

If you're a small business owner like Caroline who wants to navigate the world of finance confidently, this book is tailor-made for you. Caroline, like many entrepreneurs, realized the importance of understanding financial ratios to make sound business decisions.

Financial ratios are powerful tools that help assess a company's performance, measure profitability, and gauge financial health. This book breaks down these ratios into bite-sized concepts, provides real-life examples, and guides you through practical exercises.

Financial ratios are the secret ingredients that add flavor and insight to your business' financial health. So roll up your sleeves and join Caroline on this exciting journey as we demystify financial ratios, ensuring you can tackle financial recipes with confidence!

The Surface of Financial Ratios: What is Financial Analysis
Financial analysis is like a powerful magnifying glass that allows businesses to delve deeper into their financial data and gain valuable insights. It examines financial statements, ratios, and other metrics to understand a company's performance, profitability, and overall financial health.

Imagine Caroline, a determined small business owner who has set sail on the vast ocean of entrepreneurship. Along her journey, Caroline has realized that understanding financial analysis is crucial for steering her business in the right direction. It became her compass, guiding her through the twists and turns of decision-making.

Through financial analysis, Caroline can evaluate her business's strengths and weaknesses, identify potential risks, and spot opportunities for growth. It empowers her to make informed decisions based on concrete financial evidence rather than guesswork or intuition.

The Interior of Financial Ratios: Learning to Calculate Ratio Analysis

Step into the enchanting realm of financial ratios, where numbers come alive and weave tales that reveal the intricate details of a company's financial well-being! In this journey of discovery, we'll start by exploring the foundation of ratio analysis: ratios themselves.

RATIOS

Consider ratios as powerful tools that allow us to understand and evaluate different aspects of a company's financial performance. Ratios provide meaningful insights by comparing other financial variables and highlighting their relationships. They help us uncover hidden patterns and make informed decisions.

Liquidity

Liquidity ratios are like compasses that show a company's ability to handle short-term financial obligations. Since Caroline wants to be able to run a successful business, she needs to know some key ratios:

Current Ratio

Before Caroline bakes a cake, she has to lay out the necessary ingredients on the kitchen counter. The current ratio is like the proportion of wet ingredients (or current assets) to dry ones (current liabilities). So Caroline can calculate her current ratio (i.e., the recipe to success) by dividing the wet ingredients, such as cash, inventory, etc., by her dry ingredients, like accounts payable and short-term debts.

The equation looks like this:

"Current Ratio = Current Assets / Current Liabilities"

Generally, a current ratio of between 1.5 and 3 is perfect.

The current ratio only considers the assets that are readily available and currently owed liabilities, so it might overlook long-term obligations like paying off loans or purchasing new baking equipment, i.e., capital expenditures.

Cash Ratio

Let's zoom in on the cash ratio, a trusted sidekick for Caroline's financial journey. The cash ratio is similar to a jar of cash set aside for purchasing supplies. It represents the portion of cash on hand that can be used without the help of other assets.

To calculate the cash in the jar or cash ratio, Caroline has to divide her cash and cash equivalents by her current liabilities.

The equation is simple:

"Cash Ratio = Cash and Cash Equivalents / Current Liabilities"

When it comes to the cash ratio, a good range would be similar to having enough cash in the jar to purchase all the baking ingredients. While there is no one-size-fits-all range for the cash ratio, it should ideally be above 0.2 to 20 percent.

The downside of this ratio is that it does not consider the changes and inflation in prices, so it might become less effective with time. In addition to this, just like Caroline may miss out on the opportunity to invest in better equipment if she keeps too much cash in her jar, businesses may face limitations on capital allocation if assets are kept in cash.

Net Working Capital Ratio

Net working capital ratio is a valuable ally. The NWC ratio represents, for example, the ratio of ingredients required for baking cakes to the overall ingredients bought on credit. It measures a company's ability to meet its short-term obligations, and it is used to assess its financial health.

To calculate it, Caroline subtracts her current liabilities (i.e., money still owed to vendors) from her current assets (ingredients) and divides the result by her current liabilities.

Here's the equation:

"Net Working Capital Ratio = (Current Assets - Current Liabilities) / Current Liabilities"

As Caroline learns to wield these ratio tools, she gains insights that empower her decision-making process. But to ensure she's baking financial success, she needs to ensure that her NWC ratio lies in the positive range, or she might end up not having enough money to pay for the ingredients she needs. When it comes to the net working capital ratio, Caroline cannot measure the quality of those ingredients and how well they are managed. Just as Caroline's well-managed bakery steers clear of wastage, companies must manage and optimize their inventory.

Days Sales Outstanding

Also called the average collection period, this is a financial metric that represents the average number of days it takes for

Caroline to receive customer payment after selling a cake on credit. It measures the average number of days from the moment she sells the cake to when the payment reaches her account. DSO can be calculated by dividing the accounts receivable for a given period by the total credit sales for the same period and multiply the result by the number of days in the period. Here's what the equation looks like:

"Days Sales Outstanding = (Accounts Receivable/ Credit Sales) x Number of Days"

The lower the DSO, the faster she can collect her payments and ensure better liquidity. Using this ratio comes with a few drawbacks, including the fact that it doesn't consider the quality of the accounts receivable or seasonal variations.

Quick Ratio

The quick ratio indicates Caroline's bakery's short-term liquidity position, helping her measure her business's ability to meet its short-term obligations with its most liquid assets. For instance, if Caroline needs to make 24 cookies for a neighborhood party, she needs to first ensure whether she has the flour, milk, chocolate, and eggs to create the mix.

To utilize this ratio, you only need the following super simple formula:

"Quick Ratio = Current Assets - Inventory / Current Liabilities"

With this ratio, Caroline can determine her bakery's ability to convert liquid assets into cash to pay her short-term financial obligations. That way, if she has to bake a huge order, she can ensure she has enough flour (emergency savings) to survive!

Solvency

Solvency refers to a company's ability to meet its long-term financial obligations. It's like having a sturdy foundation that ensures the business can sustain itself and fulfill its commitments. Let's explore the key components of solvency and understand why it's crucial for every business.

Debt to Equity Ratio

Caroline uses the debt to equity ratio to find the right balance between debt and equity in her business. It's calculated by dividing the total debt by the shareholders' equity.

"Debt to Equity Ratio = Total Debt / Shareholders' Equity"

Generally, the ratio should be lower than 1, indicating a lower reliance on debt financing. While calculating this ratio, Caroline needs to remember that the metric does not consider specific timings of debt payments nor reflect the market value of equity.

Financial Leverage Ratio

Caroline knows that financial ingredients must be well-balanced, just like the right combination of sugar and flour in her recipes. The financial leverage ratio measures the amount of assets financed with debt versus those financed with equity.

"Leverage Ratio = Total Assets/ Shareholders' Equity"

The financial leverage ratio is all about balancing, so it's best to keep the ratio low (although it can vary based on industry benchmarks). But with the positives come the negatives, so this ratio's drawback is that it does not consider the timing and quality of debt payments.

Debts to Assets Ratio

The debt to assets ratio is the ratio of borrowed ingredients (liabilities) to total equipment (assets). Caroline can calculate this ratio by dividing the liabilities by the total equipment.

Here's its equation:

"Debt to Asset = Total Debts / Total Assets"

When the ratio yields a low and positive number, it represents a lower reliance on debt financing. One major downside of relying on this ratio is that it doesn't provide an accurate representation of debt payments, which can impact your financial statements. (Remember those? We learned all about them in Chapter 3.)

Fixed Charge Ratio

The fixed charge ratio is similar to Caroline's income after deducting fixed expenses from operating income. With this ratio, Caroline can determine how well her treats are helping her meet her fixed financial obligations.

Here's the magic formula Caroline needs to calculate this:

"Fixed-Charge Coverage Ratio = (EBIT + Lease Payments) / (Interest Payments + Lease Payments)"

Here EBIT means *earnings before interest and taxes*

In FCR, a ratio above 1 is desired to ensure that Caroline *can* cover her fixed charges without having to sell her favorite cookbooks. But its downside is that it does not represent accurate cash flows, so it might not be able to capture Caroline's unique cash flow dynamics.

Asset Turnover Ratio

The asset turnover ratio represents Caroline's ability to generate sales revenue from ingredients, ovens, refrigerators, and other baking equipment. In simpler words, it's the ratio of cakes sold to the ingredients and equipment used.

Here's what its equation looks like:

"Asset Turnover Ratio = Net Sales / Average Total Assets"

Although the number can vary from industry to industry, the ideal range is a higher ratio. Why? Because it represents high sales efficiency. But it's not all sunshine and rainbows; this ratio can sometimes miss the mark by failing to reflect sales' timing and the current market value of assets.

Profitability

Profitability is a vital aspect of any business, determining its financial success and sustainability. It refers to the ability of a company to generate profits from its operations. By analyzing profitability, businesses can assess their financial health, make informed decisions, and identify areas for improvement.

Gross Profit Margin

Like a skilled chef, Caroline knows that profitability starts with the right ingredients. The gross profit margin measures the percentage of revenue after deducting the cost of goods sold. Caroline can calculate it using the equation:

"Gross Profit Margin = (Revenue - Cost of Goods Sold) / Revenue"

This ratio helps her understand the efficiency of her production and pricing strategies.

Pricing Strategies: Unleashing the Profit-Packing Power of Numbers

In the captivating business world, pricing is like a well-tailored suit—it must fit just right. Caroline knows that setting the perfect price isn't just about dazzling her customers; it's about ensuring that her revenue stands tall, confidently covering the relentless onslaught of operating expenses and those persistent tax collectors who always seem to have their hands out.

With a touch of wit and a pinch of financial finesse, Caroline understands that her pricing strategy must be like a hidden treasure chest—guarded enough to secure her profitability yet enticing enough to capture the attention of her target market. By navigating this delicate dance, she can unveil the perfect price point that satisfies her customers' desires and keeps her business sailing smoothly toward long-term success.

So let Caroline's pricing strategies be your guiding light on this daring journey. Arm yourself with creativity and wit as you craft prices that ride the winds of success. Strike that perfect harmony between covering your costs and keeping customers captivated, for in this kingdom of pricing, only the bold and witty prevail. May your prices reign supreme and your profits flourish!

Net Profit Margin
Caroline realizes that true profitability takes into account all expenses. The net profit margin reveals the percentage of revenue that remains as net profit after deducting all expenses, including taxes and operating costs. Caroline can calculate it using the equation:

$$\text{"Net Profit Margin = Net Profit / Revenue"}$$

This ratio provides a comprehensive view of her business's overall profitability.

Return on Investment (ROI)

Like a savvy investor, Caroline seeks to maximize her return on investment. The ROI measures the profitability of an investment relative to its cost.

> **"ROI = (Net Profit from Investment / Cost of Investment) x 100"**

This ratio helps her assess the effectiveness of her investments and make informed decisions about future endeavors.

ROI (return on investment) is a financial ratio that measures the profitability of an investment by comparing the net profit generated to the cost of the investment. It is expressed as a percentage.

The Two Numbers That Make up the ROI Ratio Are:

1. **Net Profit from Investment:** This number represents the profit earned after deducting all relevant expenses, including operating costs, interest, and taxes. Net profit is derived from financial statements such as the income statement, which provides an overview of revenues and expenses.

Example: Caroline invests $50,000 in a small business venture. After a year, the business generates a net profit of $10,000. In this case, the net profit from the investment would be $10,000.

2. **Cost of Investment:** This number represents the total cost incurred to invest, including the initial investment amount, any additional expenses, and

transaction costs. It reflects the capital outlay required to acquire or develop the asset.

Example: In Caroline's case, the cost of her investment would be the $50,000 she initially invested in the business.

The ROI ratio indicates the efficiency and profitability of the investment. It quantifies the return generated for the cost of the investment. A higher ROI means the investment has generated a higher return than its price, suggesting a more favorable outcome. Conversely, a lower ROI indicates that the investment has yet to generate significant returns on its cost.

Limitations of ROI:

1. **It does not consider the time value of money:** ROI does not account for the fact that money earned in the future is worth less than money earned today. It assumes that the returns are received at the same time as the investment.

2. **It does not account for the investment duration:** ROI does not consider the period over which the returns are generated. It treats all investments with the same ROI equally, regardless of their time horizons.

A good range for ROI varies depending on the industry, investment type, and risk appetite. Generally, a higher ROI is desirable, but it should be compared to industry benchmarks and other similar investments to assess its relative performance.

Return on Equity (ROE)
ROE measures how well a company is using its shareholders' equity to generate profits. Shareholders' equity is the amount of money the shareholders have invested in the company plus

accumulated earnings less dividends. It is calculated as follows:

"ROE = Net Profit / Shareholders' Equity"

ROE is crucial information for any owner. A good ratio depends on many factors, your goals and your industry. A good target for a stable and established business is 10-15%. It shows that you're rewarding your stakeholders with steady returns. Make adjustments if you see numbers below these results, and if your results are higher, congratulations!

Free Cash Flow Margin

Free cash flow margin measures the percentage of revenue converted into free cash flow after deducting operating expenses and capital expenditures. It indicates the company's ability to generate cash from its operations, fund future investments, or pay dividends. A higher free cash flow margin is generally considered favorable, as it signifies a healthier financial position. FCF margin is calculated by:

"Free Cash Flow Margin = (Free Cash Flow / Revenue) x 100"

Free cash flow, as included in the formula above, can be measured by starting with operating cash flow and deducting capital expenditures. Both these figures will be presented on the cash flow statement.

In Caroline's case, as she explores investment opportunities for her business, understanding these ratios can help her make informed decisions. By analyzing her profit margins, ROI, ROE, and free cash flow margin, Caroline can evaluate the potential investments by analyzing her profitability, operational performance, and cash flow generation. She needs to consider these ratios alongside other financial metrics and industry benchmarks to assess the investment's viability and alignment with her business goals.

Caroline's intrigue in using financial analysis for her business reflects her ambition to make informed decisions that drive success. By understanding and calculating these profitability measures, she gains valuable insights into her business's financial performance, identifies areas for improvement, and paves the way for sustainable growth.

Assessing Profitability: Stakeholders' Use of Ratios for Company Evaluation and Industry Comparison

Profitability ratios are valuable tools for stakeholders to evaluate companies and make industry comparisons. These ratios provide insights into a company's financial performance, efficiency, and profitability. Let's explore how stakeholders utilize profitability ratios and consider Caroline's perspective.

Evaluating Financial Performance:

- **Gross Profit Margin:** Stakeholders assess a company's ability to generate profits from its core operations. A higher gross profit margin indicates effective cost management and pricing strategies. For Caroline, a high gross profit margin would reflect her business's ability to generate profits from goods or services sold.
- **Net Profit Margin:** This ratio measures a company's profitability after accounting for all expenses. Stakeholders, including Caroline, use it to evaluate overall profitability. A higher net profit margin indicates efficient expense management and significant profits compared to revenue.

Assessing Efficiency:

- **Return on Assets (ROA):** Stakeholders analyze how effectively a company utilizes its assets to generate profits. A higher ROA indicates efficient asset utilization and higher returns. Caroline would benefit from a high ROA, indicating that her business generates substantial profits relative to its assets.
- **Return on Equity (ROE):** This ratio evaluates a company's profitability on shareholders' equity. Stakeholders use it to gauge returns for shareholders. A higher ROE indicates that a company delivers strong shareholder investment returns. Caroline would aim for a high ROE to ensure her business generates significant returns as the owner.

Industry Comparison:

To assess relative performance, stakeholders compare profitability ratios across companies within the same industry. They can identify industry leaders, evaluate competitive advantages, and spot potential investment opportunities. For Caroline, industry comparisons provide benchmarks to measure her business's profitability and identify areas for improvement.

Considering Caroline's Perspective

As an entrepreneur, Caroline can use profitability ratios to evaluate her business's financial health and performance. These ratios offer insights into her business's profitability, efficiency, and return on investments. By analyzing her business's profitability ratios, she can identify strengths and areas for improvement and measure competitiveness. This knowledge empowers her to make informed decisions, set realistic financial goals, and strategically manage her business's profitability.

Using profitability ratios, stakeholders understand a company's profitability and can make informed investment and strategic decisions.

Diving Deeper: How to Analyze Financial Performance Using These Ratios

Imagine yourself as Caroline, a passionate baker who understands the importance of analyzing financial performance to create a recipe for success.

Like baking a delicious cake, analyzing liquidity ratios ensures you have all the necessary ingredients. The current ratio acts as your pantry, measuring your current assets (the ingredients) against your current liabilities (the recipe requirements). It ensures you have enough ingredients instantly available to meet your obligations and keep your business running smoothly.

Now let's move on to solvency ratios, the sturdy foundation of your baking masterpiece. Just as a cake needs a strong base, your business needs a solid financial footing. The debt to equity ratio evaluates the balance between debt and equity in your business's structure. It ensures you have the right proportion of ingredients to create a stable and sustainable business.

Finally, profitability ratios are like the icing on the cake, adding sweetness to your success. The gross profit margin is the delicious aroma that fills the room, indicating the profitability of each baked good. The net profit margin is the perfect level of sweetness, considering all expenses to provide a comprehensive view of your overall profitability. And the return on investment (ROI) is the cherry on top, measuring the profitability of your investments and helping you make informed decisions about where to allocate your resources.

As Caroline, you understand that analyzing these ratios is like following a tried-and-true recipe. Regularly assessing your liquidity, solvency, and profitability can whip up a financially successful business. So grab your apron, put on your baker's hat, and let these ratios guide you in creating a mouthwatering business that leaves everyone craving more. Remember, with the right financial analysis, you can bake your way to sweet success!

The Last Step: How to Make Recommendations Using Analysis

Envision yourself in the kitchen, preparing a mouthwatering cake and reaching the final stage, elevating its flavor to new heights. Similarly, when it comes to analysis, making recommendations is crucial. It's like adding the perfect frosting to your cake.

To make recommendations, carefully review your analysis findings and consider what actions can be taken to improve the situation. Identify the key areas that need attention and brainstorm specific strategies or solutions. Like adjusting the baking time or adding more flavor to your cake, your recommendations should be tailored to address specific challenges or opportunities.

Caroline has a passion for creating delectable cakes that make people smile. She spends hours experimenting with flavors and perfecting her techniques. With her creative mind and attention to detail, Caroline has become known for her extraordinary cakes that are loved by everyone who tries them. Her dedication and love for baking shine through every bite of her masterpieces.

Trend Analysis: The Secret Ingredient to Sustainable Success

Just like Caroline tracks the process of every cake she makes, she needs to examine her bakery's financial data to determine patterns, changes, and trends. It's a lot like taking pictures of her cakes through the years to see how they've evolved.

In addition, just as Caroline compares her sales to understand which items are a hit and which are not, trend analysis allows her to take a look at her financial statements, including income statement, cash flow statement, and balance sheets (if you didn't shout these names out, you need to review Chapter 3 again!) to evaluate performance over a certain period.

Through trend analysis, Caroline can determine if her sales revenue has risen like perfectly baked bread or sunk like a failed soufflé. She can also determine noticeable shifts in her financial mix due to the addition of a new pastry and what items need to be taken off the menu.

By examining these trends, business owners (and Caroline) can gain insights into their business's financial health, identify areas of improvement, and develop wise courses of action.

Industry Benchmarking: The Last Element for Financial Analysis

Industry benchmarking is similar to how Caroline compares her cupcakes with the bakery down the street. Just like she compares the rise and texture of her dough and the moistness and richness of her baked treats with other bakeries, industry benchmarking involves assessing financial performance against competitors. That way, Caroline can identify whether her cupcakes are up to par or are missing the 'wow' factor.

For instance, Caroline might compare her prices to determine if they are achieving sweeter levels of profitability than her competitors or if she needs to switch up her strategy. Besides this, she can assess her cupcake mix to understand if she's offering the right flavors or needs to introduce an amazing new one to stand out.

Overall, with industry benchmarking, Caroline can determine if her bakery is aligned with the industry standards. She can also find her strengths, i.e., her mouth-watering red velvet cake, and determine where she 'kneads' to work harder. As a result, she can improve performance and efficiency to bake sweeter, more delicious financial mixes!

Awesome! You've finished learning all about the basic financial ratios and how they contribute to understanding your business's growth and performance. Now that we've covered that, it's time to test how well you've absorbed the information through some fun and challenging exercises, along with multiple-choice and true/false questions.

Test Your Knowledge: Fun Exercises, Examples, and Tips
Questions

Q1. Review the financial statements presented in Chapter 3 and calculate the following six ratios:

1. Current Ratio
2. Debt to Equity Ratio
3. Debt to Asset Ratio
4. Net Working Capital Ratio
5. Return on Investment

6. Gross Profit Margin

Ensure that you add the calculations down below.

Response:

Q2. Although Caroline has read and made notes of the different types of financial ratios, she still finds herself stuck on liquidity vs. solvency. So explain them both, and indicate how their respective ratios apply to Caroline's bakery.

Response:

Short Questions

Q1. What are financial ratios, and why are they important? Explain in two to three sentences.

Response:

Q2. What is the return on investment (ROI) ratio?

Response:

Q3. Explain the debt to equity ratio and what would be a good result.

Response:

Q4. Explain the gross profit margin ratio and how it's helpful for a business

Response:

Q5. What is the current ratio and what would be a good result?

Response:

Multiple-Choice Questions

Choose the right option and check the answers below to verify your answers:

Q1. The quick ratio can be calculated by dividing:

    a) Current assets by total assets
    b) Current liabilities by total liabilities
    c) Total equity by total debt
    d) Current assets less inventory by current liabilities

Q2. The debt to equity ratio helps to assess:

    a) The efficiency of inventory management
    b) The profitability of a company's investment
    c) The success of marketing strategies
    d) The solvency position of a company

Q3. Businesses can use the Fixed Charge Ratio to measure

    a) The ability to generate sales from inventory
    b) The efficiency of accounts receivable
    c) The ability of profits to meet financial obligations
    d) The liquidity position of a company

Q4. The Asset Turnover ratio measures

    a) The ratio of net income to shareholders' equity
    b) Ability to generate sales from assets
    c) The ratio of net income to total assets
    d) Market's expectations of future earnings

Q5. The net profit margin ratio can be calculated by:

    a) Multiplying net profit by revenue
    b) Dividing net profit by total equity
    c) Dividing total equity by total debt
    d) Dividing net profit by revenue

True/False

Tick the right answer (p.s. Don't flip back while you solve these!):

Q1. The Cash ratio measures your company's ability to cover short-term liabilities and short-term assets.

True   False

Q2. The Leverage ratio is your company's financing coming from debt compared to equity.

True   False

Q3. The Net Working Capital ratio measures the return earned on investments relative to the cost of the investment.

True   False

Q4. The ROA ratio measures a company's ability to generate stock prices from total assets.

True   False

Q5. The Free Cash Flow Margin indicated the ability of the company to generate cash from its operations.

True   False

Answers:

Q1. 1. Current Ratio:

Current Ratio = Current Assets/Current Liabilities

Current Assets = $10,050 + $4,500 + $15,000

Current Assets = $29,550

Current Liabilities = $7,550

Current Ratio = $29,550 / $7,550

Current Ratio = 3.91

2. Debt to Equity Ratio:

Debt to Equity Ratio = Total Liabilities / Shareholders' Equity

Total Liabilities = $7,550 + $20,000 = $27,750

Shareholders' Equity= $52,000

Debt to Equity Ratio = $27,550/$52,000

Debt to Equity Ratio= 0.53

3. Debt to Asset Ratio:

Debt to Asset Ratio: Total Liabilities / Total Assets

Total Liabilities = $27,550

Total Assets = $79,550

Debt to Asset Ratio = $27,550 / $79,550

Debt to Asset Ratio= 0.35

4. Net Working Capital Ratio:

Net Working Capital Ratio = (Current Assets - Current Liabilities) / Total Assets

Current Assets = $29,550

Current Liabilities = $7,550

Total Assets = $79,550

Net Working Capital Ratio = ($29,550 - $7,550) / $79,550

Net Working Capital Ratio = 0.28

5. Return on Investment:

Return on Investment = Net Income / Total Assets

Net Income = $22,700

Total Assets = $79,550

Return on Investment = $22,700 / $79,550

Return on Investment = 0.29 or 29%

6. Gross Profit Margin:

Gross Profit Margin = (Sales Revenue - Cost of Goods Sold) / Sales Revenue

Sales Revenue = $100,000

Cost of Goods Sold = $35,000

Gross Profit Margin = ($100,000 - $35,000) / $100,000

Gross Profit Margin = 0.65 or 65%

Q2. Liquidity and solvency are both important financial concepts that provide insights into a company's financial health and stability but are distinct. While liquidity refers to a company's ability to meet its short-term obligations and ability to convert into cash without significant loss, solvency is the company's ability to meet its long-term financial obligations, indicating its financial stability and sustainability.

When it comes to liquidity, the current ratio measures the company's ability to pay off its current liabilities using its current assets. As calculated in question one, the current ratio is 3.91, which means for every dollar of liability, the bakery has $3.91 of current assets available to meet its obligations. On the contrary, the debt to equity ratio indicates the solvency ratio that measures the proportion of a company's financing that comes from debt compared to equity. As calculated, Caroline's bakery's debt to equity ratio is 0.53, which means she has $0.53 of debt for every dollar of equity.

Short Answers

Q1. Financial ratios are quantitative measures used to assess a company's financial performance and health. They offer in-depth insights into a business's operations, profitability, efficiency, liquidity, and solvency. Financial ratios are important because they allow companies to evaluate their financial position, make informed decisions, and compare performance to industry standards.

Q2. The ROI ratio measures the profitability of an investment relative to its cost, i.e., the ratio of the net profit from an investment by the cost of the investment. It helps to assess the effectiveness and profitability of investment decisions.

Q3. The debt to equity ratio measures the proportion of a company's financing from debt divided by its equity. Its formula is as follows: "Debt to Equity Ratio = Total Debt / Shareholders' Equity." A good result would be less than 1.

Q4. The gross profit margin ratio is a metric that represents the profitability of a company's core operations by calculating the percentage of revenue. It also helps to determine a company's ability to generate profits from products/services.

Q5. The current ratio is the proportion of current assets to current liabilities, and a good ratio is between 1.5 and 3.

Multiple-Choice

Q1. d

Q2. d

Q3. c

Q4. b

Q5. d

True/False

Q1. False

Q2. True

Q3. False

Q4. False

Q5. True

Tips
- Review your financial ratios on a monthly or quarterly basis so you can respond to issues in a timely manner.
- Compare your current ROI to your ongoing business goals on a regular basis to determine what works well and what needs improvement.

- Calculate EBITDA alongside financial reports to determine profitability. *(EBITDA = Net Income + Interest + Taxes + Depreciation&Amortization)*

Now that you've finished the tricky exercises and learned must-know tips and tricks, we've got a muffin to help you celebrate! Once you've finished that, remember to throw the paper bag in the nearest trashcan and roll up your sleeves. We're about to jump into the world of financial risks, so grab your coffee or tea as we learn to combat potential risks and challenges!

CHAPTER 5

Managing Risks and Challenges with Confidence

While financial knowledge is critical to running a successful business, it's incomplete without understanding the risks and challenges. From market volatility and regulatory changes to abrupt downturns and unprecedented events, there's a lot business owners need to learn.

But fear not! While there are a plethora of risks and challenges in the financial world, there are also endless ways to manage them effectively. With the proper knowledge and a robust mitigation plan, you can ensure your business rises like yeast.

In this chapter, we'll examine the different financial risks and challenges Caroline can face when running her business. Besides this, we'll discuss how she can measure and mitigate these risks to avoid burning her cakes:

The Basics of Financial Risks: Terms You Should Know

Before Caroline can avoid financial risks, she needs to know the basic terms and phrases. Let's start by discussing some financial risk-related words:

Economic Downturn

One sales period can vary from another. An economic downturn refers to a period of reduced consumer spending and economic activity, resulting in lower demand for Caroline's scrumptious treats.

For instance, Caroline's bakery may notice reduced customer demand due to an economic downturn as customers cut back on luxury pastries and opt for more affordable options, such as store-bought cookies.

Competition
Competition refers to the presence of other bakeries or food establishments selling similar products to the Sweet Caroline Bakery. If Caroline faces extreme competition, she'll likely find herself in the middle of a price war, customer retention struggles, and the need to differentiate.

For instance, if there's another bakery down the street offering cupcakes and brownies, it can pose a threat to Caroline's bakery, which sells similar (but more delicious, of course) baked goods.

Natural Disasters
Based on where you establish your business, you might experience unpredictable natural threats, such as floods, fires, or hurricanes that can disrupt your operations.

For instance, if Caroline wants to expand her bakery to Texas, she'll have to consider the potential challenges if a flood occurs. This could cause equipment loss and the temporary closure of her bakery.

Business Environment Change
If you've spent two minutes in the business world, you know that it's an ever-evolving and dynamic landscape. That means Caroline needs to stay up to date with new rules and regulations, shifts in consumer trends, and advancements in bakery-related technology.

For instance, if the government introduces new and stricter health and safety rules regarding bakery-related equipment, Caroline may need to buy different equipment or supplies to comply with these standards.

Human Error
Businesses can also suffer financial risks due to a mistake or accident caused by individuals. This could include incorrect baking times, mishandling of products, or improper use of equipment.

The Basics of Financial Challenges: More Terms to Remember
Caroline now knows all the most important financial risk words, but what about the *challenges?* Worry not, we've got you covered!

Overspending
Overspending is exactly what it sounds like: It's when a business exceeds its budget, spending more than it generates.

Poor Cash Flow Problems
Poor cash flow occurs when a business experiences a shortage of available cash to meet its immediate financial obligations. For instance, if Caroline experiences slow sales due to an economic downturn, she might face difficulties in paying her suppliers or employees.

Poor Account Collection
Poor account collection involves the challenges of collecting payments from customers who have purchased desserts on credit, leading to a delay in receiving the expected cash flow and hurting the bakery's financial stability.

For instance, if Caroline extends credit to the café next door for wholesale orders, but it delays payments, it can harm her bakery's financial health.

Declining Profits

Declining profits involve a decrease in the bakery's net income over time, such as increased competition, rising ingredient costs, and a decline in customer demands. If, for instance, Caroline's bakery experiences a decrease in sales volume due to not maintaining price competitiveness, its profits may decline.

Late Payments

Late payments occur when customers and clients fail to make their payments within the agreed-upon timeframe. For instance, if Caroline bakes a custom cake for her customer's birthday, but they fail to make timely payments, she could suffer from cash flow constraints.

Increasing Debts

Increasing debts, as the name suggests, refers to the accumulation of financial obligations owed by a business. This can occur due to borrowing money or taking a loan to fund operations.

For example, if Caroline wants to add home delivery services to her business, she might take out a loan, which adds to her debts, causing a higher debt burden.

Bankruptcy

Bankruptcy is a financial situation where a bakery is unable to repay its debt, which means it is legally declared insolvent. This can lead to the closure of a business (sometimes forever) and liquidation of assets.

For instance, if Sweet Caroline Bakery takes a huge loan that it's unable to pay, Caroline might have to face bankruptcy.

Employee Layoffs

Employee layoffs occur when a business is forced to reduce its workforce to cut costs and meet changing business conditions. For example, if Caroline experiences an economic downturn, she might have to lay off employees to control expenses and maintain financial viability.

Inventory Issue

If you didn't catch it from the name, inventory issues involve financial challenges related to managing and controlling a business's stock of ingredients, finished products, and supplies. For instance, Caroline may unexpectedly run out of flour and baking powder due to inaccurate inventory tracking.

Taking Action: How to Detect Financial Risks and Challenges

Now that Caroline has learned the basic terms related to financial risks and challenges, she can move on to the next step, which is taking action.

Just like Caroline needs proper guidelines to start making a new recipe, she needs to know *how* she can detect financial risks to protect herself and her company.

Step 1: Review Financial Statements

The first step to detecting financial risks is to review your financial statements (which we've already learned about!) To achieve this step, Caroline must:

- Conduct regular reviews of her financial statements, which includes balance sheets, income statements, and cash flow statements.
- Analyze key financial ratios (which we covered in the previous chapter), including return on investment and gross profit margin, to identify potential risks.

- Look for any unusual or unexpected fluctuations in revenue, expenses, and profitability, such as declining profits.

Step 2: Monitor Cash Flow

It's no secret that businesses need to generate a consistent cash flow to enjoy success. But to identify how well her cash flow is performing, Caroline needs to track and monitor it.

Wondering how? Here are the steps Caroline should take to monitor her cash flow:

- Track cash inflow and outflow regularly to ensure a healthy cash flow.
- Conduct weekly, quarterly, and monthly cash flow projections to identify potential pitfalls and surpluses.
- Monitor industry trends and market conditions to identify potential opportunities and risks that can impact cash flow.
- Seek advice from financial advisors (which we will discuss in the upcoming chapters) to gain in-depth insights.

Step 3: Stay Updated with Industry Trends

Monitoring cash flow is not enough to ensure sustainable revenue or a successful business. Caroline needs to go beyond tracking her cash flow and learn to stay up to date with the latest industry trends.

Here's how:

- Stay in the know about the latest industry trends, regulations, and market conditions by monitoring publications, trade associations, magazines, and articles.

- Attend relevant conferences, workshops, and seminars (like Caroline did in Chapter 2) to network with like-minded professionals and gain knowledge of the latest trends and challenges.
- Engage in open-ended discussions with industry professionals and fellow bakers to share experiences and exchange information on financial risks and detection.

Step 4: Track and Control Expenses

Once Caroline knows how to monitor industry trends, she can move on to tracking her expenses by following these steps:

- Maintain a detailed record of all the expenses related to baking operations, including ingredient costs, equipment maintenance, and overhead expenses.
- Regularly review and analyze the expenses to identify areas of excessive spending, cost inefficiencies, and potential hits.
- Implement cost control measures without compromising the quality of ingredients (or the yummy desserts), such as negotiating favorable contracts, exploring bulk purchasing ideas, or replacing low-selling products.

Step 5: Consult with a Financial Advisor

While following these steps will help Caroline take charge of her business finances, it's unlikely that she'll *never* run into another financial challenge. So if she's struggling to identify financial risk, Caroline can do the following:

- Seek professional advice from a financial advisor specializing in the baking industry.

- Discuss financial goals, challenges, and concerns with an expert advisor to learn about potential risks.
- Partner with a proficient financial advisor to develop customized risk management strategies tailored to the bakery.
- Review and update her financial plan regularly to adapt to changing business circumstances.

The Final Solution: Waving Goodbye to Financial Risks and Challenges by Mitigating Them

After learning how to detect financial risks, the natural step is to mitigate them. Just like how Caroline can add a little water or milk to fix a dry batter, she needs to learn the secrets to curbing financial risks.

Fortunately, it's not as difficult as it sounds. Here are the ins and outs of mitigating financial risks to ensure a stress-free business:

Take Control of Expenses

Before anything, Caroline needs to learn how to take control of her expenses. This involves:

- Implementing a budgeting system to track and control expenses
- Conducting regular cost analyses to identify and curb areas of potential overspending
- Engaging in supplier negotiations and optimizing production processes to ensure the best pricing and minimal waste

Optimize Cash Flow Management

It goes without saying that you can't run a business without a healthy cash flow. To ensure a successful business based on a sustainable cash flow, Caroline needs to:

- Maintain a cash flow forecast to anticipate potential shortfalls and take proactive measures to mitigate them.
- Offer incentives for customers to make timely payments, including providing discounts for early payments.
- Implement an effective inventory management plan to avoid overspending on inventory.

Boost Profitability

If Caroline wants to grow and expand her business, she needs to learn how to ensure profitability by:

- Analyzing pricing strategies and adjusting them to ensure maximum profitability.
- Evaluating and optimizing operation efficiency, exploring new revenue streams, and conducting market research to adapt product offerings.
- Enhancing marketing and advertising efforts to attract new and retain old customers.

Manage Debt Effectively

Debt is the quickest way for a business to fail. So to avoid suffering this fate, Caroline must follow these steps:

- Develop a comprehensive debt management plan to prioritize and pay off debt.
- Negotiate with lenders for a more favorable repayment term or potentially reduce interest rates.
- Implement effective cost control measures to generate funds for debt repayment.

Navigate Financial Distress

There's always the risk of disaster lurking in the shadows, whether it's excessive debt or natural disaster. To safeguard the bakery, Caroline needs to have a plan in place, which involves:

- Developing a detailed financial recovery plan to address debts and achieve financial stability.
- Exploring financial assistance programs for small businesses and startups.
- Implementing a revised business strategy to meet changing needs and improve sustainability.

Incorporate a Financial Cushion
Similar to the step above, Caroline needs to ensure she has a financial cushion to power through a disaster. This should include:

- Allocating a portion of profits to build an emergency fund.
- Establishing a reserve to navigate financial downturns and unforeseen circumstances.

Negotiate Contracts
Here's a secret: You don't have to give up premium ingredients if you can negotiate! Here's what Caroline needs to do:

- Establish strong relationships with suppliers to negotiate favorable pricing and terms.
- Regularly review contracts to negotiate better terms based on business growth and changes.

Look for Insurance Coverage
Insurance is crucial to protect yourself against financial losses, whether for your bakery or your car. For this step, Caroline needs to:

- Assess her bakery's insurance needs and collaborate with an agent to discover the appropriate coverage.

- Monitor and update insurance policies to ensure the insurance aligns with growing business needs.

Seek Professional Assistance

It's always a good idea to talk to a professional advisor to mitigate financial risks. Here's how this works:

- Reach out to industry associations, trade groups, and mentorship programs to seek guidance and support.
- Join peer networks or forums to connect with like-minded professionals and fellow business owners facing similar challenges.

Now that you've made it to the end of this chapter, you now officially know all the basics of financial risks and challenges, how to detect them, and ways to mitigate them. That means you're now ready to power through the exercises and activities!

Test Your Knowledge: Fun Exercises, Examples, and Tips
Questions

Q1. Caroline is now ready to tackle financial risks and challenges. But to get started, she needs to know the different methods to detect and combat potential financial risks and challenges in her bakery. What do you believe these include?

Response:

Q2. How do financial forecasting and budgeting contribute to mitigating financial risks related to Caroline's bakery?

Response:

Short Questions

Q1. What is financial risk management?

Response:

Q2. How can a business identify and detect financial risks and challenges?

Response:

Q3. Name one basic financial challenge and how it could be mitigated?

Response:

Q4. What role does cash flow management help in mitigating financial risks?

Response:

Q5. Why must businesses stay informed about industry trends?

Response:

Multiple-Choice Questions

Q1. A Financial challenges includes:

a) Generating good cash flow
b) Buying a new oven your business does not need
c) Paying down your debts on time
d) Increasing profits from a new cupcake line

Q2. Financial statement review helps businesses:

a) Monitor industry trends
b) Expand product offerings
c) Spot unusual trends in expenses
d) Track cash inflow and outflow

Q3. Poor account collection can cause:

a) Increased customer satisfaction
b) Improved cash flow
c) Lower profits
d) Poor supplier terms

Q4. Consulting with a financial advisor helps businesses:

a) Stop overspending
b) Handle employee layoffs
c) Make late payments
d) Develop custom risk management strategies

Q5. Tracking and controlling expenses involves:

a) Monitoring inventory
b) Regularly reviewing and analyzing expenses
c) Hiring new employees
d) Conducting customer surveys

True/False

Q1. Boosting profitability involves increasing expenses by 2%.

True   False

Q2. Financial forecasting helps in anticipating potential financial risks by projecting future revenues, expenses, and cash flows.

True   False

Q3. Effective cash flow management is crucial for mitigating financial risks.

True   False

Q4. Financial forecasting only focuses on past financial performance.

True   False

Q5. Analyzing financial statements once in a while can help you detect potential risks.

True   False

Answers:

Q1. Detecting potential financial risks and challenges requires utilizing various methods and tools, which aids in timely identification. For starters, Caroline needs to regularly review and analyze her financial statements, including balance sheets, income statements, and cash flow statements. That way, she can gain in-depth insights into her bakery's financial health, allowing her to spot potential risks.

In addition, Caroline needs to track and monitor financial ratios like gross profit margin, ROI, and liquidity, allowing her to highlight areas of concern and reveal trends that indicate potential risks.

Besides this, Caroline may need to collaborate with a financial advisor or consultant specializing in the baking industry. These professionals bring expertise and experience, offering valuable insights and guidance in risk detection.

Q2. Financial forecasting and budgeting offer a forward-looking view of a business's financial performance, allowing business owners to anticipate and solve financial challenges and take measures to mitigate them. This involves projecting future revenues, expenses, and cash flows based on historical data, market trends, and other relevant factors.

Through forecasting and budgeting, Caroline can identify potential risks, such as declining costs, cash flow shortages, and increased debt, whereas by budgeting, she can translate financial figures into an actionable plan by setting specific targets for revenues, expenses, and profitability.

Short Answers

Q1. Financial risk management is the process of identifying, assessing, and mitigating potential risks that can impact the financial stability and performance of a business.

Q2. Businesses can identify potential financial risks and challenges by reviewing financial statements, analyzing key financial ratios, monitoring cash flows, and seeking professional advice.

Q3. Natural disasters are a financial challenge and could be mitigated by purchasing sufficient insurance that would cover your business in case of loss or business interruption from a natural disaster.

Q4. Effective cash flow management ensures the availability of sufficient funds to meet financial obligations and enable proactive measures.

Q5. This helps businesses stay informed about industry trends and market conditions, resulting in the adoption of strategies and mitigation of risks.

Multiple-Choice

Q1. b

Q2. c

Q3. c

Q4. d

Q5. b

True/False

Q1. False

Q2. True

Q3. True

Q4. False

Q5. False

Tips

- Don't give up! Keep fighting to combat your financial issues.
- Don't panic and remain calm. Consider your options, create a plan, and execute it properly.
- Be open and honest with your team, vendors, and customers. Remember to build trust and seek support.

Awesome, you now know the secrets to detecting and mitigating financial risks. In addition, we're halfway through the book! Here's delicious custard to celebrate our learning journey. Once you're done, grab your apron, for we're about to jump into the wondrous world of fraud protection.

CHAPTER 6

Protecting Your Small Business from Fraud

We've all been there: receiving a suspicious email with a vague offer and a request to fill out a lengthy form with *all* your personal information. In a similar fashion, several days ago, Caroline received an email from a vendor she'd never heard of before.

Puzzled yet intrigued, Caroline opened the email only to find the "vendor" asking for a hefty payment for all the things she doesn't even own! As her business instincts kicked in, Caroline embarked on a new journey to uncover the truth behind this suspicious invoice.

After some research (and five coffees later), involving thorough research, scouring the Internet for any reviews related to the company, and some credible information on the vendor, Caroline learned that fraud can happen even to small businesses.

While Caroline's curiosity had been piqued, she also became aware of the fact that she doesn't know a lot about detecting and avoiding business fraud. If that sounds like you, this chapter is a *must* for you! Today, we'll follow Caroline on her journey to learning the ins and outs of fraud and how business owners can wave goodbye to them.

The Power of Accounting: How It Helps Business Owners Stay Away from Fraud

Harnessing the power of accounting, just like learning the art of baking, allows individuals to protect themselves from fraud by providing them with the knowledge, skills, and tools to identify and prevent business fraud. Here's how Caroline (and you) can utilize accounting to prevent fraudulent activities.

Understanding Financial Statements

Just like Caroline uses recipes to understand precise measurements, accounting education enables her to comprehend and analyze financial statements. By studying her balance sheets, income statements, and cash flow statements, Caroline can detect any irregularity, inconsistency, and unusual patterns that indicate fraudulent activities.

Besides this, equipping yourself with financial knowledge makes it easy for you to identify red flags to conduct further investigation, if necessary.

Internal Control Systems

Learning accounting allows Caroline to discover the secret ingredients to creating robust internal control systems that help protect her assets, ensure accurate financial reporting, and minimize the risks of fraudulent activities. By understanding these complex components and principles, Caroline can implement preventive measures.

Fraud Risk Assessment

Business owners need to identify areas of vulnerability within their industries to evaluate the likelihood and impact of potential fraud. By conducting a thorough fraud risk assessment, Caroline can take proactive measures to prevent fraud from occurring.

Forensic Accounting Skills

Forensic accounting focuses on investigating financial fraud and detecting financial irregularities. By learning the secrets of forensic accounting techniques, users can identify fraud indicators, trace financial transactions, and build a robust case against fraudulent activities.

Auditing Skills

Learning the principles of auditing helps Caroline to examine her financial records, critically evaluate internal components, and conduct independent assessments of her organization.

Similar to how her meticulous baking skills allow her to examine each layer of a cake to ensure it's baked to perfection, Caroline's business instincts help her identify irregularities and raise concerns about potential fraud.

Fraud Detection Techniques

With a solid foundation of fraud detection tools and strategies, Caroline can identify unusual patterns and deviations that signify fraudulent activities, just as she can detect a subtle off-taste!

Starting at the Basics: What Are the Different Types of Fraud?

Before Caroline can start fighting business fraud, she needs to learn the different types of fraud.

BILLING FRAUD

Fraudulent businesses often use deceptive practices to manipulate invoices and billing processes for personal gains.

In billing fraud, a business might overcharge, create fictitious invoices, misrepresent services, or alter payment details to trick Caroline into thinking she owes a third-party organization or individual money. Take, for instance, last week when Caroline received a supply invoice from a new vendor. Trusting the legitimacy of the vendor, she proceeded to make the payment without realizing that they had deliberately inflated the price per bag on her invoice. As a result of his deception, Caroline paid a higher amount than what was initially agreed upon, allowing the vendor to pocket the funds they did not earn, thereby committing billing fraud.

To detect billing fraud, Caroline would have had to carefully scrutinize her past invoices, cross-reference the invoices with authorized purchase orders, and ensure the legitimacy of the vendors. These protection layers would have helped Caroline identify potential red flags and avoid fraudulent activities from hurting her business.

EMPLOYEE FRAUD

Employee fraud refers to misconduct by employees that involves the misuse or theft of their employer's resources for personal gain. Red flags that could indicate employee fraud include sudden employee lifestyle changes, unexplained business financial difficulties and frequent unrecorded business cash transactions. Some common examples include:

- **Payroll fraud** - involves inflation of hours worked or submission of false reimbursements that hurt Caroline's bakery's revenue and integrity. It can involve the deliberate manipulation and misappropriation of funds related to employee compensation, ranging from the creation of ghost employees to the submission of false reimbursement claims. Perpetrators of payroll fraud seek personal financial gain and excess amounts by exploiting weaknesses and gaps in payroll processes and controls.

For instance, Caroline's pastry chef Karen, motivated by greed, might decide to commit payroll fraud by altering her timesheets by adding extra hours. By doing this, Karen fraudulently increases her paycheck, deceiving Caroline and forcing her to pay extra by committing payroll fraud.

Furthermore, payroll fraud can have severe repercussions on Caroline's business, resulting in financial losses, damage to employee morale, and legal implications. Detecting and preventing payroll fraud requires the implementation of strong internal controls and thorough verification of payroll data. Thus, to protect her business against payroll fraud, Caroline needs to regularly review and reconcile payroll records, closely monitor employee information, and promptly investigate suspicious activities.

- **Expense reimbursement fraud** – submitting fictitious or inflated expense reports
- **Embezzlement** – stealing incoming payments or cash belonging to the company
- **Inventory theft** – stealing physical inventory, assets, or equipment and selling them
- **Data theft** – stealing proprietary data , intellectual property, or customer information
- **Invoice fraud** – creating fake vendor invoices and pocketing payments
- **Credit card abuse** – making unauthorized personal purchases on credit cards
- **Bribery and kickbacks** – secretly accepting payments to award business or contracts
- **Financial statement manipulation** – falsifying accounts and books for bonus payouts or hiding losses

- **Check fraud** - illegally altering or forging checks for personal gain, encompassing a range of deceptive practices like unauthorized signature changes, counterfeit checks, and unauthorized access to bank accounts.

For example, imagine a fraudulent baker named Kevin entering the Sweet Caroline Bakery. With ill intentions, Kevin steals a blank check from a customer's bakery order and alters the check by adding to the amount to withdraw funds from the customer's bank account without authorization. By deceitfully changing the payee name and amount, Kevin commits check fraud, causing financial repercussions for Caroline's bakery, resulting in financial losses and damaged relationships.

The bank also plays a critical role in identifying and combating fraud by implementing robust systems and signature verification processes.

Here are some other ways your business can protect itself against employee fraud:

- **Background checks** – conduct them on new hires to uncover any red flags in their history
- **Vacations** – require mandatory vacations and rotate duties to add scrutiny of each employee's activities
- **Access** – institute policies that limit access to sensitive information and physical assets
- **Technology** – install surveillance cameras, access control systems, and inventory management software
- **Audits** – perform regular audits and spot checks for both physical and digital transactions
- **Hotlines** – encourage whistle blowing and provide anonymous hotlines for reporting suspected fraud

- **Security** – enforce strict cybersecurity protocols like access restrictions and password policies
- **Training** – train employees on ethical behavior and risks of fraud
- **ERP** – implement ERP and accounting software with automated fraud detection
- **Inspections** – conduct surprise inspections of employee workspaces and remote offices
- **Prosecute** – prosecute any fraud to the fullest extent of the law
- **Insurance** – maintain insurance policies that cover employee theft and fraud liability

CREDIT CARD FRAUD

This type of fraud involves the unauthorized use of someone else's credit card information, such as fraudulent transactions, stolen credit card details, counterfeit cards, and unauthorized online purchases.

Most perpetrators of credit card fraud exploit vulnerabilities to unlawfully obtain goods, services, and financial gains. Take, for example, Caroline's employee Greg, who works at the checkout counter, secretly stealing customers' credit card information by using a skimming device while processing their payments and using these details to make unauthorized processes. Credit card fraud can hurt Caroline's business, leading to financial losses, identity theft, and damaged credit scores.

Therefore, to protect herself against credit card fraud, Caroline needs to encourage individuals to exercise caution when sharing their credit card information, regularly monitor their credit card statements, and promptly report suspicious activities. In addition, to ensure security, Caroline can implement secure payment gateways or two-factor authentication.

CYBER ATTACKS

Cyber attacks related to cyber fraud typically involve hackers compromising computer systems, networks, or data in order to steal sensitive information for financial gain or extortion. Some examples of cyber attack fraud are:

- **Phishing scams** - type of online cyber attack where cybercriminals leverage deceptive techniques to trick individuals into revealing sensitive information, including usernames, passwords, and financial details. Typically, these scammers impersonate trusted entities, such as a reputable organization or bank, to gain the victim's trust and manipulate them into willingly providing confidential data.

  Take, for instance, Caroline's secret cake recipe, aka the envy of the whole town! Caroline receives an email from a suspicious but seemingly well-known baking association, claiming they want to recognize her delicious cakes by featuring it in a prestigious magazine. While the email seems genuine due to the association's logo and a request to click on a 'confirm link' to participate and provide confidential essentials, this can impact her business significantly!

  Without knowledge of phishing scams, Caroline might end up feeling eager to seize this opportunity crafted by cybercriminals who can access her secret recipes and personal data!

- **Malware** - used to intercept credit card data, as we discussed above

- **Corporate databases** - hacked to steal customer information like social security numbers to create fake accounts and identities for fraudulent transactions
- **Ransomware** – encrypts an organization's critical data and hackers demand a ransom payment in order to decrypt it
- **Denial-of-service attacks** – take down retail websites before big sales events to extort payments from the company
- **Money transfer and financial systems** – compromised to manipulate funds transfer data and steal money
- **Synthetic identities** – created using stolen PII to apply for loans and credit cards that default for profit
- **Brokerage accounts** – hackers gain access to manipulate trading platforms and algorithms for financial gains

Some specific steps that can be taken to mitigate cyber attacks include the following:

- **Install Security Software** – safeguard data against unauthorized access and malware using antivirus, firewall, and intrusion detection systems
- **Regularly Update Software** – to avoid breaches, keep operating systems, applications, and plug-ins up-to-date with the latest security patches
- **Implement Strong Passwords** – enforce strong passwords and multi-factor authentication
- **Backup Data** – regularly backup critical business data to help mitigate the loss of data due to a breach
- **Train Employees** – educate your employees specifically about cyberattacks, phishing scams,

breaches, and other cyber threats to minimize the risk of falling for such attacks.

- **Encrypt Sensitive Data** – Encrypt sensitive data stored on databases and portable devices

The key to combating employee fraud is combining employee fraud protection strategies. Stay diligent! We will discuss more general mitigation steps in the following sections.

Slowing Down: Learning the Secrets Behind Forensic Accounting and Auditing

Discovering Forensic Accounting Techniques

Forensic accounting techniques involve meticulously examining financial data to uncover any hidden lumps of irregularities. Forensic accountants, equipped with their investigative whisks, utilize various techniques like data analysis, financial reconstruction, and interviews to knead through financial records, transactions, and documents.

With the help of forensic accounting, businesses can reveal any financial dough that doesn't rise to the occasion. Their objective, much like baking the perfect cake, is to provide a comprehensive and accurate analysis of financial information that can withstand the heat of dispute and internal investigations.

Understanding the Basics of Auditing Skills

Before we dive into the part where Caroline learns to take action against business fraud, she needs to know the essentials of auditing skills. Just like how bakers follow a precise recipe, auditors methodically examine financial statements and records to ensure they are well-measured and adhere to accounting principles, regulations, and industry standards.

For this, businesses leverage a systematic evaluation to test internal controls, certify financial accuracy, and perform substantive testing, just like Caroline uses her well-calibrated oven to bake cakes to perfection. That way, they can serve up an unbiased opinion on the financial reporting, much like Caroline's delicious cakes satisfy her clients and showcase her bakery's financial credibility to stakeholders.

Being Proactive: What Should You Do When You Suffer from Business Fraud?

When Caroline receives a vague email from a suspicious username, what should she do to protect herself from a malicious attack?

Easy: She needs to address her business issue by taking steps to assess the situation and protect her interests. Here's how it works.

Step 1: Notify the Bank

Caroline needs to immediately notify her bank about the fraudulent practices she's encountered. Once she reports the fraud to the relevant authorities, she can move on to the next step.

Step 2: Freeze or Block Accounts

When it comes to business fraud, time is *everything*. So, without wasting any time, Caroline needs to take swift action to freeze and lock any accounts involved in fraudulent activity.

Step 3: Gather the Necessary Evidence

Caroline needs to collect the information relevant to the fraudulent transactions. This includes invoices, contracts, receipts, emails, and any other records that can serve as proof.

Once Caroline documents the transactions, she can build a solid case against the fraudulent activity.

Step 4: Contact Legal Consultants
When Caroline runs into a baking-related issue, she reaches out to her superior chefs to identify ways to solve the problem. In the same vein, when her bakery faces fraud, she needs to seek legal professionals who can guide her through the legal process.

Step 5: Initiate Claims and Chargebacks
Caroline she needs to initiate the dispute resolution process for any fraudulent activity. This involves submitting a claim backed by heavy evidence. In addition, she must collaborate with the relevant organizations to combat and rise above these fraudulent activities.

Step 6: Monitor and Protect Your Credit Card
Last but not least, Caroline needs to go through her financial statements and credit reports. That way, she can identify any inconsistencies and unusual patterns to detect further fraudulent activities. A credit monitoring service can also help with this.

Ensuring You're One Step Ahead: Ways to Protect Your Small Business
Small business owners must take the proper steps to protect their businesses from facing fraud.

Let's now discuss the different steps small business owners can take to keep their companies safe.

Know Your Vendors

Small business owners need to know and evaluate their vendors. Before you partner with a new vendor, take the time to assess and research different vendors thoroughly.

Remember to research your desired vendor's reputation, check references, evaluate their reviews and ratings, and ensure their vision and culture align with yours. That way, you can ensure the vendor is reliable and trustworthy.

Use Strict Payment Authorization Procedures

Businesses must implement a rigorous system of 'financial measurements' to ensure that only authorized transactions go through.

Furthermore, Caroline needs to establish clear protocols for payment approvals involving multiple verification steps. The result? Reduced risk of unauthorized and fraudulent activities and a safe and sustainable business.

Besides this, small business owners like Caroline can go one step further to ensure improved authorization by verifying the accuracy of their invoices and maintaining a system of checks to prevent any irregularities in their financial mix.

Secure Financial Information

In the baking world, safeguarding your secret recipes is your one-way ticket to long-term success. Similarly, Caroline needs to protect her business's financial information as if it were a magic potion.

To protect her business from fraud, Caroline might encrypt sensitive information, regularly back up her data on a different disk or device, and employ firewalls to protect her coveted recipes from potential breaches.

Moreover, Caroline, and you, need to ensure your financial information is *always* up to date to fortify your financial security and prevent business fraud.

Educate Your Employees on How to Recognize Fraud

You don't close your eyes, cross your fingers, throw a little flour in the sky, and hope you will magically transform into a world-famous baker overnight. Trust us, it takes years of learning, training, and lots and lots of trying and failing before you can reach baking mastery.

In the same vein, you can't stick a "Fight Against Fraud" poster in your bakery and hope all your employees will learn to recognize the warning signs. Instead, you need to provide thorough training to enhance their financial baking awareness, making them vigilant and able to identify red flags.

Furthermore, with appropriate training, your employees can learn how to detect unusual transactions, suspicious mail or texts, and requests for sensitive information. You'll also promote open dialogue, encourage them to raise concerns without hesitation, and foster a healthy and fraud-proof culture within your workplace.

Monitor Your Accounts

Small business owners need to regularly monitor their business accounts to minimize the risk of fraud.

Remember to review your bank statements, financial reports, and transaction logs and utilize innovative technology (or hire professional assistance) to track your accounts regularly and avoid fraud. By monitoring your accounts diligently, you can quickly identify any discrepancies and address issues in a timely fashion, thus minimizing potential damage.

By implementing these five strategies, Caroline can fortify her bakery against potential business threats. Similar to how Caroline meticulously follows each step in her recipes to achieve a perfect product, small business owners must take the right measures to protect their businesses and allow them to flourish.

Now that you've learned all about the different types of business fraud, how you should act if you're a victim of fraud, and the recipe for protecting your business against it, you're now ready to move on to the fun part: the exercises and activities!

Test Your Knowledge: Fun Exercises, Examples, and Tips
Questions

Q1. Take a look at the following email Isabella, the assistant manager, received in Caroline's bakery:

Subject: Exclusive Wholesale Opportunity-Limited Time Offer!

Sender: [Fraudulent Name]

Email Address: [fraudster@emailprovider.com]

Dear Isabella,

I represent a well-established wholesale supplier with an exclusive offer that I believe would be of great interest and beneficial to your business. We have recently come across your bakery's reputation for high-quality products and are impressed by your success.

Our business is pleased to extend an exclusive opportunity for you to purchase our premium, world-class ingredients at amazingly discounted rates. Our inventory includes a plethora of essential products, ranging from top-notch flour and milk to imported chocolates and rare spices, all of which can make your bakery more attractive and enhance its offerings, which translates to more customers and even more revenue!

To take advantage of this exclusive wholesale deal, please respond to this email with your contact details and the estimated quantity of required products immediately. Once we receive your response, we will share our pricing details and shipping information.

But remember, this offer is only valid for a limited time! So, we encourage you to act swiftly, or you might miss out on a once-in-a-lifetime opportunity. We look forward to establishing a long-term partnership with your bakery and providing you with top-notch ingredients to help you create the best-baked goods in town.

[Fraudster's Name]

Determine whether this email is real or not and provide evidence to back your claim.

Response:

Q2. Caroline's Bakery recently experienced a cyberattack that led to significant data loss. How do you believe she can protect her bakery from another cyber fraud and data breach?

Response:

Short Questions

Q1. What is fraud, and why does it matter for small businesses?

Response:

Q2. How do internal controls help small businesses minimize the risk of fraud?

Response:

Q3.In what ways can a small business protect itself from phishing scams?

Response:

Q4. How can business owners identify potential red flags for employee fraud?

Response:

Q5.What steps should you take to secure financial transactions and payments?

Response:

Multiple-Choice Questions

Q1. What is business fraud?

    a) A government tax incentive
    b) A legal and fair business practice
    c) A deceptive behavior for personal gain
    d) A legitimate investment opportunity

Q2. How could a con artist contact your business:

    a) Phone
    b) Email
    c) Mail
    d) All of the above

Q3. Which of the following is a common cyber fraud threat for small businesses?

a) Phishing emails
b) Secure password management
c) Regular data backups
d) Strong encryption

Q4. Should small businesses invest in insurance to protect against fraud-related losses?

a) No, fraud insurance is unnecessary for small businesses
b) Yes, insurance coverage is essential for financial protection
c) Insurance doesn't cover fraud-related losses
d) Small businesses don't need insurance for protection

Q5. How does employee training prevent fraud in small businesses?

a) By telling employees it's okay to engage in fraudulent activities
b) By raising awareness and promoting ethical behavior
c) By undermining security measures and internal controls
d) By making employees vulnerable to cyber threats and emails

True/False

Q1. Fraud only occurs in large corporations, not small businesses.

True   False

Q2. Fraudulent vendors are not a concern for small businesses as they already deal with reputable suppliers.

True   False

Q3. Business owners should always be cautious of unsolicited communication from unknown and suspicious sources, like phone calls, emails, and mail.

True   False

Q4. Small businesses are not susceptible to data breaches and cyberattacks.

True   False

Q5. Phishing emails are a prevalent cyber fraud threat that small businesses need to be aware of.

True   False

Answers:

Q1. Based on the information provided, there are several red flags that suggest this email is likely a fraud. Here's how we know this is a fraudulent attempt:

- **Suspicious Email Address-** The sender's email address appears unprofessional and suspicious. Authentic businesses typically use official email addresses containing their company's domain.
- **Generic Greetings-** The email starts with an informal and generic greeting without mentioning Isabella's full name or position. Most businesses/wholesale suppliers that reach out for a business opportunity personalize their email.
- **Unspecified Wholesale Supplier-** The email does not provide any information on the wholesale supplier, which hints at a fraudulent attempt. A legitimate supplier would include their company's

name, contact information, and official website to capture interest.

- **High Praise but no Specifics-** The email praises Caroline's bakery without any reference or detail. An authentic business would dive into specific information and why it matters to them.
- **Urgency-** Another huge red flag is that the email puts pressure on Isabella by mentioning the exclusivity and urgency of the offer, increasing the risk of prompt action without running a verification check.
- **Request for Immediate Response-** Lastly, the email urges Isabella to respond with her contact details and order without even mentioning Caroline's bakery in the email.

Q2. Caroline can enhance her protection against cyber fraud and data breaches by following these steps:

- **Install Security Software-** Caroline can safeguard her data against unauthorized access and malware using antivirus, firewall, and intrusion detection systems.
- **Regularly Update Software-** To avoid breaches, Caroline must keep her operation systems, applications, and plugins up to date with the latest security patches.
- **Implement Strong Passwords-** Caroline must enforce intricate passwords and multi-factor authentication to up her security game.
- **Back up Data-** Regularly backing up critical business data helps mitigate the impact of data loss due to breach.
- **Train Employees-** Educate your employees about cyberattacks, phishing scams, breaches, and other

cyber threats to minimize the risk of falling for such attacks.

- **Encrypting Sensitive Data-** Lastly, she must encrypt sensitive data stored on databases and portable devices.

Short Answers

Q1. Fraud is deceptive behavior carried out to gain an unfair advantage or cause harm. It's a concern for small businesses as it can cause financial losses and damage their reputation.

Q2. Internal controls are procedures and checks that help businesses prevent and detect fraud by segregating duties and implementing secure processes.

Q3.The best way to protect a business against phishing scams is to educate employees, encourage skepticism, and implement strong email security measures.

Q4. Red flags that indicate employee fraud include sudden lifestyle changes, unexplained financial difficulties, and frequent unrecorded cash transactions.

Q5. The best way to secure financial transactions is to use secure payment gateways that require multi-factor authentication and regularly reconciling accounts.

Multiple-Choice

Q1. c

Q2. d

Q3. a

Q4. b

Q5. b

True/False

Q1. False

Q2. False

Q3. True

Q4.False

Q5.True

Tips

- Run extensive employee background checks before hiring a new candidate.
- Install a robust firewall on your computer systems and encourage employees to change their passwords every 60 to 90 days.
- Invest in ID theft and fraud insurance to protect your business against fraud.

Awesome! You now know about protecting your small business against fraud and data breaches- this calls for a yummy scoop of ice cream. Gobble it up fast, for we're about to dive into the magical world of budgeting and forecasting (P.S. There's a little math, so you might want to grab your calculator!)

CHAPTER 7

The First Step to Strategic Financial Planning: The Secret World of Budgeting and Forecasting

J ust like Caroline doesn't like to try a new baking recipe without first checking detailed steps and a vivid picture, she's not thrilled at the prospect of running a bakery without step-by-step guides and in-depth budgets. And although she wants to plan her financial activities to create a successful cake mix, there's one problem: Math is *not* her strong suit! Since budgeting and forecasting are all about determining expected income from her delectable treats while accounting for necessary expenses like flour, eggs, milk, sugar, and *so* much more, she's always struggled to create budgets and forecasts. Luckily, we're about to unravel the complexities of forecasting and budgeting to reveal that they're not really as challenging as they seem.

Ready or not, it's time we learn how budgets and forecasts are the ingredients missing in your financial mix and how not having them can hinder your ability to reach new levels. Let's find out how Caroline can use these tools.

The First Step: Setting SMART Goals to Kick-Start Your Budgeting and Forecasting Journey

Every baker knows how indispensable a clear and detailed recipe is to baking. In the same vein, a well-written budget based on SMART goals can provide clarity, accountability, realistic expectations, and time management.

With SMART goals, Caroline can track progress, hold herself accountable, align financial objectives, and set time-bound goals. But wait—what exactly are SMART goals?

Let's take a look at a step-by-step guide.

Specific- Just like specific ingredients and measurements are crucial to baking the perfect cake, setting specific goals helps Caroline define her desired financial outcomes. For instance, if she wants to reduce ingredients costs by 10 percent, she would have to focus on that aspect of her budget to select the right goods.

Measurable- When baking a batch of brownies, measurements, and timing are *everything* to ensure yummy (and not burnt) results. In the same sense, measurable goals are crucial for tracking progress. Take, for instance, Caroline wants to increase her orders by 20 percent. By setting this goal, she can measure the actual increase and adjust sales and marketing strategies accordingly.

Achievable- Just like you can't bake a cake out of thin air, it's important to set goals within your capabilities and limits. For instance, if Caroline sets the goal to expand to ten new locations, she might actually be setting herself up for disappointment. On the contrary, aiming to open one new storefront can be more feasible and realistic.

Relevance- Similar to how Caroline wouldn't throw garlic in her cake, it's vital for businesses to set relevant budgeting goals. That way, Caroline can ensure that her financial objectives align with her vision and mission. For example, Caroline sets a new goal to increase her revenue from specialty and seasonal cakes, thus aligning with her focus on catering to birthday and wedding parties and expanding her reach.

Time-Bound- What's the worst way to bake a cake? Putting it in the oven and forgetting to take it out at the right time! Save your cakes from being burnt by creating time-bound goals. These goals create a sense of urgency, encouraging you to stay on track, keep improving, and make adjustments that align with your strategies and objectives. For instance, when Caroline starts creating a batch of cookies, she ensures she preps the right ingredients at the right time and then leaves the batter in the oven for just the ideal amount to ensure her cookies are baked to perfection!

The 'Why': Reasons Why SMART Goals Are the Key to Success in Budgeting and Forecasting

SMART goals are crucial for Caroline, allowing her to set realistic and achievable goals while working toward the bigger picture. With these objectives, she can determine *what* she wants and *how* she plans to rise to success.

Moreover, they help her keep moving forward, despite the small disasters along the way. Here's why setting SMART goals is essential for *every* small business owner.

SMART goals **offer clarity and focus** in the budgeting world. These goals help her outline the financial outcomes she *needs* to achieve and the necessary actions.

The best part of setting SMART goals is that **they're measurable**! Caroline can track her progress and evaluate her performance to assess how close she is to achieving her goals and what ingredients she's missing.

SMART goals play a critical role in **strategic and realistic planning**. Recently, Caroline added an in-house delivery team, allowing customers to order delicious treats from the comfort of their homes. But to achieve this, she needs to align her financial goals with her business strategy.

Budgeting vs. Forecasting: How Do These Two Terms Differ?

Budgets are similar to a recipe, representing *what* you want to achieve. On the other hand, forecasts can be likened to estimating how your baked goods will turn out, i.e., expectations.

We know: It sounds a little confusing. So take a deep breath; we're about to dive into the differences.

Budget aka The Recipe- Financial budgets are a lot like the recipes that tell Caroline the precise measurements of ingredients and the anticipated costs for a particular period, typically around a year. Just like how these recipes guide her to create her town's favorite treats, budgets aid in creating a robust financial framework with the expected income, expenses, and financial plan. That way, she can manage her bakery's finances and hit her financial objectives.

Forecast aka The Baked Goods- Conversely, forecasts are similar to the expected outcomes of the baked goods. Before mixing a new batter, Caroline checks how the cupcakes will look at the end. Similarly, forecasts indicate where your company is going based on performances and evaluations, typically between 2-5 years. But to create accurate estimates, Caroline has to predict future sales, costs, and profitability based on historical data and market trends. Forecasts must be updated based on market and other relevant factors changes on a rolling basis.

Getting Real: The Steps to Creating an Awesome (and Functional) Budget and Forecast

Now that Caroline's learned the difference between the financial budget and forecast, she's ready to bake a mean business plan. Here are the steps she'll take.

Step 1: Preheating the Oven

Much like the baking process starts by preheating the oven, the budgeting and forecasting creation begins by gathering revenues. Once done, she has to review and identify revenue sources, including sales of cakes, pastries, and cookies and expenses like ingredients and utilities.

Step 2: Finding the Right Ingredients

Similar to how Caroline judges what her cake will look like based on the recipe, business owners need to estimate revenue based on historical data and market trends. But before she can start performing complex calculations (hint: it's not *that* difficult), she needs to determine the right ingredients, like customer preferences and market conditions.

Step 3: Separating the Ingredients

Before baking a cake, Caroline needs to separate her wet and dry ingredients. In the same vein, she needs to categorize her expenses based on fixed and variable components.

Fixed components remain constant regardless of volume, including rent and insurance, whereas variable expenses do fluctuate based on volume, such as flour and sugar.

Step 4: Measuring the Ingredients

You can't bake the world's tastiest cakes based on random measurements; you need to follow precise measurements. In the same vein, business owners must estimate varying categories based on the driving trends and factors.

For instance, the volume of cakes baked can impact variable expenses. So Caroline can estimate ingredient costs based on projected sales volume.

Step 5: Kneading the Dough

After measuring the ingredients, it's time to mix and knead the dough, i.e., creating a budget and forecasts based on estimated revenue and expenses. Caroline can calculate her net profit/loss by subtracting expenses from revenue.

Step 6: Taste-Testing

Just like Caroline taste-tests her cookies, she has to provide her budget and forecasts to stakeholders and investors for review. They might ask her to adjust her financial batter to ensure it aligns with her long-term goals.

Step 7: Baking to Perfection

To bake her financial cake to success, Caroline has to incorporate adjustments based on stakeholder feedback. The result? She gets the perfect recipe for a mouth-watering cake.

But the work doesn't end there. She must keep reviewing her budget and forecast, usually on a monthly or quarterly basis, to ensure they're *always* accurate and up to date.

That's all you need to know to get started with killer budgets and forecasts. But (and we're sure you know this by now) the journey to a new accounting sphere doesn't end with just gaining knowledge. Instead, it's important you test yourself with fun but tricky questions to fortify your knowledge, so let's get started:

Test Your Knowledge: Fun Exercises, Examples, and Tips Questions

Q1. The current rent expense line item on the income statement from this year is $2,000 per month. According to the current lease agreement, the rent increases per annum by four percent. What should the budget be for monthly rent expenses for next year?

Response:

Q2. Take a look at Caroline's budget for 2023:

Revenue:

Retail Sales- $280,000

Wholesale Sales- $40,000

Total Revenue- $320,000

Expenses:

Cost of Goods Sold- $100,000

Marketing and Advertising- $25,000

Bakery Staff Wages- $100,000

Rent and Utilities- $25,000

Equipment, Maintenance, and Repairs- $15,000

Administrative Expenses- $10,000

Total Expenses- $275,000

Net Income = Revenue − Expenses

$320,000− $275,000= $45,000

Forecast:

Assumptions:

1. Retail Sales growth rate: 2% per year

2. Wholesale Sales growth rate: 5% per year

3. Cost of Goods Sold remains stable

4. Bakery Staff Wages increase by 1% per year

5. Rent and Utilities increase by 2% per year

6. Marketing and Advertising expenses increase by 5% per year

7. Equipment Maintenance and Repairs remain stable

8. Administrative expenses increase by 2% per year

Using these assumptions, Caroline can project her budget for the upcoming year:

Revenue:

Retail Sales: $285,600 (2% increase)

Wholesale Sales: $42,000 (5% increase)

Total Revenue: $327,000

Expenses:

Cost of Goods Sold: $100,000

Marketing and Advertising: $26,250 (5% increase)

Bakery Staff Wages: $101,100 (1% increase)

Rent and Utilities: $25,500 (2% increase)

Equipment Maintenance and Repairs- $15,000

Administrative Expenses- $10,200 (2% increase)

Total Expenses: $278,050

Net Income= Revenue - Expenses = $48,950

Based on the above-mentioned budget and forecast, explain the following income ratios and discuss if you believe it is or is not on a healthy path to meet Caroline's goals:

- Gross Profit Margin

- Net Profit Margin

Also, discuss how she can ensure she stays on a healthy path to long-term financial success.

Response:

Short Questions:

Q1. What are budgeting and forecasting?

Response:

Q2. How do budgeting and forecasting complement one another?

Response:

Q3. How does budgeting help with financial goal setting?

Response:

Q4. Why do you need to review and tweak budgets and forecasts periodically?

Response:

Q5. What is the time frame of a budget? How does it differ from a forecast?

Response:

Multiple-Choice Questions

Q1. The primary purpose of budgeting is:

a) Tracking historical financial data
b) Planning and controlling financial activities
c) Calculating sales and marketing campaigns
d) Analyzing return on investment

Q2. Forecasting is the process of:

a) Getting your favorite baking supplies
b) Determining real-time financial results
c) Projecting future financial outcomes
d) Auditing balance sheets

Q3. The first step of budgeting is:

a) Gathering financial data
b) Monitoring actual performance
c) Allocating resources
d) Setting financial goals

Q4. Which of the following is **not** a major component of a budget?

a) Sales forecast
b) Balance sheet
c) Cash flow statement
d) Income statement

Q5. S.M.A.R.T. goals represent the following:

a) The expected revenue and expenses for a certain period
b) The difference between budgeted and actual cash flows
c) Specific, realistic, achievable and measurable goals for a certain time period

d) The financial performance of a company at a specific period

True/False

Mark the appropriate answer based on your newly-learned knowledge:

Q1. Budgeting only focuses on tracking historical financial data.

     True   False

Q2. Forecasting involves projecting future financial outcomes based on historical data and trends.

     True   False

Q3. Budgeting and forecasting are separate processes without any interdependence.

     True   False

Q4. Budgeting and forecasting both focus on short-term financial planning.

     True   False

Q5. Cash flow plays a key role in predicting the timing and amount of cash inflow and outflow.

     True   False

Answers:

Q1. You can solve this as follows:

The current monthly rent expense is $2,000

Annual rent increase: 4%

Annual rent increase = current monthly rent expense * (annual rent increase percentage /100)

Annual rent increase = $2,000 (4/100)

Annual rent increase = $80

Total rent expense for next year = current monthly rent expense + annual rent increase

Total rent expense for next year = $2,000 + $80

Total rent expense for next year = $2,080

Budget for monthly rent expense for next year = total rent expense for next year/12 months

Budget for monthly rent expense for next year = $2,080/12

Budget for monthly rent expense for next year = $173.33

Q2. We can calculate the budget as follows:

Gross Profit Margin = Gross Profit = Revenue -Cost of Goods Sold

Gross Profit = $327,000 - $100,000

Gross Profit = $227,000

Gross Profit Margin = (Gross Profit / Revenue) x 100 Gross Profit Margin

Gross Profit Margin = ($227,000 / $327,000) x 100 Gross Profit Margin

Gross Profit Margin = 69.42%

Net Profit Margin = (Net Income / Revenue) x 100 Net Profit Margin

Net Profit Margin = ($48,950 / $327,000) x 100 Net Profit Margin

Net Profit Margin = 14.97%

Caroline's budget reflects that she will enjoy a gross profit margin of 69.42%, which indicates that for every dollar of revenue generated, she will retain 69.42 cents. Thus, her gross profit margin suggests that she is effectively managing production costs and pricing her yummy treats competitively.

In addition, she is budgeting for a net profit margin of 14.97%, which means that after deducting the bakery's expenses, she will retain up to 14.97 per dollar of revenue generated. This ratio also shows that Caroline can control her operating expenses efficiently while generating a high profit.

Since the gross profit margin and net profit margin are both healthy, it indicates that Caroline's bakery is on the right path to hitting its business goals. But to ensure success and consistent growth, she might have to compare her margins with industry benchmarks and the bakery's historical performance.

Moreover, to maintain a healthy and positive financial journey, she should monitor costs, discover opportunities for cost optimization, focus on operational efficiency, and assess her strategies. Besides this, she might have to review and analyze her financial statements and explore marketing strategies that can contribute to increased revenue and profitability.

Short Answers

Q1. Budgeting is the process of creating financial plans that represent the income and expenses of a specific period. On the other hand, forecasting is the process of predicting future financial outcomes based on market trends, historical data, and other factors.

Q2. Budgeting and forecasting complement one another by providing a comprehensive financial picture. While budgeting focuses on allocating resources for a particular period, forecasting helps to look beyond and predict future outcomes. Together, they help business owners plan and adjust financial issues.

Q3. Budgeting helps in financial goal setting by providing a proven framework for allocating resources and ensuring effective spending. With a well-written budget, business owners can set SMART goals to measure performance, focus on specific targets, and track progress.

Q4. It is crucial for business owners to review and adjust budgets and forecasts regularly to reflect up-to-date market conditions, business objectives, and other circumstances. By updating monthly to quarterly, you can ensure accuracy, avoid potential issues, and make necessary adjustments along the way.

Q5. Although the time frame for a budget can vary based on needs and preferences, they typically range from quarterly to a fiscal year. On the contrary, forecasts tend to last for longer than a year, usually over 2-5 years.

Multiple-Choice

Q1. b

Q2. c

Q3. d

Q4. b

Q5. c

True/False

Q1. False

Q2. True

Q3. False

Q4. False

Q5. True

Tips

- Prepare for multiple budgets and forecast scenarios using a rolling model (updated at least quarterly).
- Consider factoring in a small amount of cushion in forecasts and budgets to account for unexpected events.
- Before you create any budget and forecast, ensure that you've clearly defined your goals and gathered up-to-date data.

Yay! You've completed another chapter's challenging exercises and examples; here's a yummy sundae to help you celebrate. But don't get too comfortable; we're about to talk about 'taxes' (we know: shudder). The good news is you'll learn that taxes aren't all that difficult!

CHAPTER 8

Treading on Uncharted Territory: All You Need to Know about Taxes and Compliance

Imagine if the Sweet Caroline Bakery started making cakes without eggs; it would destroy Caroline's reputation as an expert baker and hurt her ability to produce high-quality and delicious treats. In the same manner, compliance with tax law helps Caroline fulfill her tax obligations and preserve her credibility.

By ensuring compliance, Caroline can flatten out any discrepancies, showcase a dedication to ethical practices, and demonstrate responsibility in the kitchen and out of it. On the other hand, non-compliance can lead to various cake-tastrophes, including tainting your reputation and causing hefty legal fines.

But it's not all dark skies and gloom. The truth is that tax requirements and compliance aren't as hard as most people believe. You only need to do a little reading and have a lot of patience to understand the laws and ensure compliance. And there's one secret ingredient you can use to further ease your task (hint: it starts with t and ends with an r and has "ax prepare" in the middle!).

So brush off the crumbs from your apron; it's time we rise to the occasion like freshly baked bread.

At a Glance: The Basics of Tax Requirements and Compliance

Just like Caroline needs to understand the fundamental ingredients and techniques before she rolls up her sleeves and starts kneading, it's essential to understand the basics of tax requirements to ensure a sweet financial journey.

Yes, you guessed it! We're about to measure and mix the different ingredients that make up the tax requirements and compliance batter.

Income Tax

Income tax is the core of your financial obligations. This type of tax is imposed on all the money you earn, including investment, wages, salaries, and self-employment.

Like all business owners, Caroline has the responsibility to accurately report and pay tax. If not, she might find herself in trouble and with no way out.

Sales Tax

All businesses that sell products to customers are required to collect sales tax. It is percentage-based and included at the point of sale. Typically, sales tax help fund public services, so why not contribute to it?

VAT Tax

Value added tax (aka VAT) is a consumption tax that businesses are required to apply at each stage of their production and distribution process. It is a common form of tax in many countries outside of the US, primarily the EU, UK, India, Canada, and Mexico.

VAT tax incrementally increases the costs of goods/services passing through the supply chain. Ultimately, the final consumer bears the burden of VAT.

Since Caroline adds value to her raw ingredients, if her business was outside the US, she would charge VAT on their value. Besides this, she adds value to her cakes by providing a convenient location, packaging, and marketing, meaning she would also charge VAT on their value.

Property Tax
Every time Caroline rents a new commercial space or purchases a delivery van or an oven, she has to pay property tax. If you're like her and have been paying this without knowing what it means, here's a quick explanation.

Property taxes are implemented on the value of land, buildings, and real estate properties. So when Caroline pays her landlord for renting kitchen space, the property tax is passed on to the local government.

Employment Tax
If you didn't quite catch it from the name, employment taxes are levied on activities related to employment, including payroll, social security, and Medicare taxes. Caroline deducts a certain amount from her employees' wages to pay their portions of these taxes, but she has to calculate and remit the money to the head chef, aka the government.

Direct Taxation
Direct taxation represents the taxes imposed on individuals (like Caroline) or entities (her bakery) that are responsible for paying them. These include income and corporate taxes, where Caroline has to pay a portion of her profits to tax authorities.

Indirect Taxation
Governing authorities impose taxes on goods and services that are indirectly passed on to the end consumer. Indirect taxation includes sales and value-added taxes that are levied

on the goods and services you or your customers purchase. For instance, if Caroline goes shopping for flour and eggs, she'll have to pay indirect taxes on them.

The Magic Ingredients for Taxation Success: Learning the Essential Components

It's no secret: To create an accurate and reliable income tax return, you need to know its essential components. Here's a brief explanation of some of the main features.

Income

Just like Caroline can't bake her world-class cupcakes without flour, you can't create reliable tax returns without mentioning income. This section represents the total money earned within a year from multiple sources, including wages, self-employment, or even investment.

Deductions

Deductions reduce your taxable income, like business expenses, startup costs, health insurance premiums, employee benefits, etc. Tax deductions can lower the amount of taxable income.

Adjusted Gross Income

Adjusted Gross Income (AGI) is gross income less certain deductions..

Standard Deduction

The standard deduction is a preset amount that is a reduction to taxable income. Taxpayers can use this if they do not have enough expenses to itemize deductions.

Credits

Credits represent the direct reductions on your taxability, allowing you to reduce the amount of tax you owe. For instance, research and development tax credit, earned income tax credit, work opportunity tax credit, and employer-provided child care credit.

Forms and Schedules
Documents like Form W-2 (in the US) provide necessary information to the governing body. The amount of forms, filing dates, and official bodies can vary from state to state and country.

Compliance with Tax Laws
While filing your taxes, it's essential to ensure you comply with all the relevant tax laws and regulations. Just like Caroline needs to carefully follow the steps of a recipe to create her divine red velvet cookies, businesses must check official government websites to ensure they're up-to-date with tax changes.

The last thing your business needs is a penalty because you missed a new taxation rule!

Tax Payments
Making estimated tax payments in advance will keep you from running into tax-related issues and penalties. This section details the taxes you might pay throughout the year, including estimated tax payments.

Signatures and Deadlines
Signatures and deadlines are the icings on top of your cake, ensuring you meet your state/country's tax laws. Just like Caroline *needs* to deliver her yummy cakes at the right time, business owners need to sign and submit their tax returns before the deadline to ensure compliance with the tax laws.

The best part is you can sign them electronically or physically!

How Long Should You Keep Records?

Business owners need to retain financial records to meet tax requirements and compliance standards. Generally, it's best to keep records of your financials for three years, including receipts, bank statements, invoices, and expense records. Why? Because these provide evidence of your cash outflow and inflow and empower you to claim deductions on tax returns. For accounting purposes, a good rule of thumb is at least seven years. These time periods are offered as a guide. Please check with your tax or accounting advisor.

But it gets better! Just like how following a recipe step by step makes it easy to create a delicious cake, keeping a record of your finances makes it easy to track financial transactions, identify expenses, and accurately report income. That means you can rely on your well-organized financial recipes to create a delightful taxation mix!

Recordkeeping and Documentation

Recordkeeping and documentation are all about creating a well-kneaded foundation for a well-baked recipe. Here's how it all works.

Recordkeeping

Recordkeeping is like a well-organized pantry, helping you keep track of all the financial ingredients and transactions related to your baking operations.

Just like how Caroline keeps track of how much flour, bags of sugar, and oil is left, she needs to update her financial records to create a clear picture of her income and expenses. The last thing she needs is a missing bag of flour, leading to losses!

Documentation

On the contrary, documentation involves gathering the necessary financial information to run your business and keep in compliance with government regulations. The process can involve collecting sales receipts, bank statements, purchase invoices, and a whole lot of other relevant paperwork.

But the good news is a little paperwork can take you a long way to financial success and tax compliance.

Reporting and Payment Deadlines

Tax Requirements	US Reporting and Payment Deadline	England Reporting and Payment Deadline
Income Tax (Individual)	April 15th	January 31st
Income Tax (Business)	March 15th	9 months after accounting periods
Sales Tax	Varies based on state and local jurisdiction	N/A
VAT	N/A	Quarterly or monthly reporting and payment
Property Tax	Varies based on local jurisdiction	N/A (council taxes are levied)
Employment Tax	Quarterly due dates	Monthly or quarterly

Just like Caroline can't bake all the treats in her bakery, run marketing campaigns, and take care of the finances, you may not be able to or even want to take care of all your taxes on your own. That's why you need to learn how you can access professional help. Let's now discuss how you can find help when filing taxes and ensuring compliance.

Getting the Help You Need: Where to Find Assistance to Ensure Compliance

No matter how much you learn about taxes, it can still be confusing. If you find yourself in a bothersome jam, you can find someone to ask for assistance. Professional tax preparers can help you navigate the complexity of tax laws and compliance.

Accountant

Accountants are trusted experts specializing in financial matters. They provide guidance, prepare tax returns, and ensure tax compliance to help a business's finances stay organized.

Tax Preparers

Tax preparers specialize in tax returns, and they can help you prepare the necessary steps to comply with tax laws.

Tax Software

Tax software can perform automated calculations, avoid potential errors, and generate required tax forms. But if you are still trying to grasp the reins of the tax world, you might prefer working with a tax preparer.

Government Agencies

Businesses can check in with government agencies like tax authorities to seek guidance, access forms, and look into updates on tax regulations.

That's all about how you can seek help when filing taxes. Tax preparers can help you file your taxes and determine errors, but they can also tell you the secrets to avoiding tax problems.

Playing Safe: Effective Ways to Avoid Tax Problems (Forever)

No one likes tax and compliance issues! Luckily, Caroline is very ready to wave goodbye to tax problems for a lifetime.

Step # 1: Always Measure Your Ingredients

If you *really* want to avoid tax issues (who doesn't?), you need to organize your records. Just like you measure the ingredients precisely for baking, you must maintain your financial transactions like income, expenses, and invoices.

You can go one step further and create sweet financial statements (psst... we learned this in Chapter 3. Don't remember? Have a quick review!).

Step # 2: Always Follow Your Recipe

The easiest way to ruin a cake is to throw the recipe aside and add ingredients without consideration. In the same way, if you fail to stay up to date with tax deadlines, you might end up with legal penalties and issues.

On the contrary, by following due dates for filing income tax and sales returns and other relevant forms, Caroline can ensure a perfect end result.

Step # 3: Seek Assistance from Certified Professionals

What do you do when you're two minutes away from a baking disaster? You ask your pastry chef for assistance! Just as they can guide Caroline through intricate baking techniques, a tax professional or tax preparer can help you navigate tax laws.

Now that you've learned the secrets to doing taxes quickly and efficiently, you need to ensure you've *actually* grasped this knowledge. Don't worry; we've got you! Here are examples and exercises to help you identify whether you can sort out your upcoming taxes.

Test Your Knowledge: Fun Exercises, Examples, and Tips
Questions

Q1. In Chapter 1, we learned the business structure of Sweet Caroline Bakery. Based on that information, identify the tax requirements to help ensure she stays compliant and doesn't miss any information.

Response:

Q2. Take a quick look at the following tax return:

Name: Caroline

Address: XYZ Anything Street, Sometown,

Social Security Number: XXX-XX-XXXX

Filing Status: Single

Income:

Baked Goods Sales Revenue: $70,000

Catering Service Income: $30,000

Total Income: $100,000

Deductions:

Cost of Ingredients: $25,000

Equipment Expenses: $3,000

Rent and Utilities: $13,000

Employee Wages: $30,000

Advertising and Marketing Expenses: $3,500

Total Deductions: $74,500

Adjusted Gross Income: $100,000 - $74,500 = $25,500

Standard Deductions: $12,950 (for single filers in 2022)

Taxable Income: $25,500 - $12,950 = $12,550

Now identify and explain the essential components of this tax return.

Response:

Short Questions

Q1. What are tax laws? Explain in two to three sentences.

Response:

Q2. Why is tax compliance crucial for business owners?

Response:

Q3. Explain income and sales tax. How are they different?

Response:

Q4. What do you think is the main difference between tax credits and deductions?

Response:

Q5. What is the deadline for filing income tax returns?

Response:

Multiple-Choice Questions

Test your knowledge by ticking the right answer:

Q1. Which of the following comes under direct taxation?

a) Sales tax
b) Value-added tax
c) Property tax
d) Excise tax

Q2. The purpose of tax laws is to:

a) Provide guidelines for tax professionals
b) Promote tax evasion
c) Discourage compliance with government regulations
d) Ensure fairness and equity in taxation

Q3. Tax credits directly:

a) Reduce taxable income
b) Increase taxable income
c) Reduce tax liability
d) Reduce tax rate

Q4. What happens if you fail to file a tax return by the due date?

a) Late payment fees
b) Audits
c) Penalties and fines
d) Nothing

Q5. Which of the following is not a common component of tax returns?

a) Personal information
b) Income and deduction details

c) Tax payment information

d) Employment history

True/False

Solve the following by marking the right answer:

Q1. Taxes are mandatory payments imposed by the government on individuals and businesses.

True   False

Q2. Sales tax is an example of indirect tax imposed on the sale of goods and services.

True   False

Q3. Tax compliance refers to selectively choosing tax laws and regulations to follow and report according to.

True   False

Q4. Filing a tax return is mandatory for all individuals, regardless of their income level.

True   False

Q5. Tax deductions reduce your taxable income, resulting in lower tax liabilities.

True   False

Answers:

Q1. To ensure Caroline stays compliant with tax requirements while running an LLC or sole proprietorship, she needs to handle these items:

- Obtain an EIN
- Select the right tax filing status
- Calculate her estimated quarterly tax payments

- Cover self-employment tax
- Consider state and local taxes
- Comply with sales tax collection and reporting
- Maintain her record-keeping and documentation
- Do her annual tax return filing
- Take her tax deductions and credits
- Consult a tax professional

Q2. Here's a closer look at the essential components of the tax return:

Personal Information:

This section includes the personal details about the taxpayer, aka Caroline, such as her name, address, and Social Security number. This information is essential to governmental authorities for identifying the taxpayer and ensuring correct tax returns.

Filing Status:

The filing status indicates Caroline's marital status and family situation, which can impact her tax rates and deductions. For instance, the tax rates on single and married people are different.

Income:

Income includes the money Caroline (taxpayer) earns during the tax year, regardless of the source, whether self-employment and investment or rental income. In the provided tax return, Caroline has two income sources: her baked goods sales and catering service.

Deductions and Adjusted Gross Income:

Deductions indicate the expenses that the taxpayer can subtract from their total income to identify their adjusted gross income. In Caroline's tax return, there are five deductions, including the cost of ingredients, equipment expenses, rent and utilities, employee wages, and advertising and marketing expenses.

Moreover, her adjusted income calculated in the tax return is $25,500, which she calculated after subtracting her total deductions from her total income.

Standard Deduction:

The standard deduction is a government-regulated amount and is subtracted before calculating the taxable income. Since Caroline identifies as 'single,' her deduction is $12,950. Note it will vary by tax year.

Taxable Income:

Lastly, the taxable income refers to the amount subject to taxation, which is $12,550, based on Caroline's tax return.

Short Answers

Q1. Tax laws are regulations and statutes implemented by the government that determine rules and regulations for taxation. Through tax laws, you can understand how taxes are levied and collected.

Q2. Tax compliance is crucial for ensuring that businesses meet their legal obligations and responsibilities. It helps to maintain the tax system and helps you avoid potential penalties and legal issues.

Q3. Income and sales taxes are taxes imposed by the government, but they vary based on how they are applied. Income tax is levied on your income, including wages, salaries, and rental income, whereas sales tax is imposed on the sale of goods and services.

Q4. The primary difference is that tax credits reduce the amount of tax owed, whereas tax deductions decrease the taxable income.

Q5. The deadline for filing income tax returns varies from country to country and individual circumstances. So you'll have to check in with your state and federal laws to determine the deadline.

Multiple-Choice

Q1. c

Q2. d

Q3. c

Q4.c

Q5.d

True/False

Q1. True

Q2. True

Q3. False

Q4. False

Q5. True

Tips

- Consult with a tax professional to determine your tax obligations. Please note that this book does **not** provide tax advice.
- The tax obligations of a business vary based on the type of business and jurisdiction. So consult a tax professional to identify which laws apply to you.
- Keep your personal and business expenses separate. If the IRS believes you have mixed the two accounts, they might start looking at your personal accounts.

Wipe the sweat off your forehead, and here's a brownie to help you feel good about learning and excelling at the basics of taxes. Now that you've crossed that bridge, we're about to dive into the exciting world of accounting software. So let's discover how accounting software works.

CHAPTER 9

Streamlining Finances and Unleashing Efficiency with Accounting Software

Caroline's excitement is palpable as she embarks on a journey to discover the power of accounting software. She understands that leveraging technology in managing her finances will simplify her tasks and pave the way for financial success.

Caroline, a passionate entrepreneur and small business owner, has always been committed to the success of her venture. As she continues navigating the intricacies of running her business, she realizes the critical role of efficient financial management in driving growth and profitability.

We will delve into the world of accounting software, shedding light on its immense benefits and exploring some of the top options available for small businesses like Caroline's. By leveraging technology and embracing accounting software's capabilities, Caroline aims to simplify her financial processes, gain better control over her finances, and make informed decisions that propel her business forward.

Harnessing the Power of Accounting Software: What Is It?

Accounting software is a digital tool designed to streamline financial management processes, allowing businesses to efficiently handle tasks such as bookkeeping, invoicing, budgeting, and reporting. With its user-friendly interface and automation capabilities, accounting software simplifies complex financial tasks, saves time, and provides accurate insights into a business's financial health.

By automating manual tasks and providing real-time data, accounting software empowers businesses like Caroline's to make informed decisions, identify areas for cost savings, manage cash flow effectively, and maintain compliance with financial regulations. With its intuitive interface and robust features, accounting software transforms financial management from a burdensome chore into a streamlined and efficient process, setting the stage for enhanced productivity and success.

Unlocking Financial Success: The Best Accounting Software for Small Businesses

As Caroline embarks on her journey to find the ideal accounting software, she discovers a range of options tailored to cater to the unique needs of small businesses. Let's explore some of the top contenders that can revolutionize Caroline's financial management practices:

Making the Perfect Financial Accounting Choice: Cloud vs. Desktop Accounting Software

Businesses should choose between cloud and desktop accounting software based on their unique requirements. We will provide a quick overview of their differences.

The primary difference between cloud and desktop accounting software is accessibility. With a cloud-based platform, you have the flexibility to access financial data anytime, anywhere. But unlike these tools, desktop accounting software offers better control over financial data and offline access.

Besides this, cloud-based accounting software provides exceptional collaboration and multi-user access. With these platforms, Caroline can add her (relevant) employees to enjoy real-time collaboration and easy access. On the contrary, desktop software offers poor collaboration opportunities but better customization options.

So if you *really* want to choose the perfect financial accounting software, you have to consider your business needs and identify which of the following platforms best matches them.

FreshBooks:
FreshBooks is a popular accounting software that offers a range of features specifically tailored for small businesses. Its intuitive interface, cloud-based accessibility, and robust invoicing capabilities make it a favorite among freelancers, consultants, and service-based entrepreneurs.

FreshBooks also seamlessly integrates with popular payment gateways, enabling convenient and secure online transactions. With its mobile app, Caroline can manage her finances on the go, ensuring that she gets all the critical updates and invoices.

Pros:
- User-friendly interface with easy navigation
- Comprehensive invoicing features for efficient client billing
- Time tracking functionality for accurate project management
- Seamless integration with third-party applications
- Mobile app for on-the-go financial management

Cons:
- Limited inventory management capabilities

- Somewhat limited reporting features compared to other options

Intuit QuickBooks:

Intuit QuickBooks is well-established accounting software that has been a trusted name in the industry for years. It offers a wide array of features, making it suitable for businesses of all sizes. With its robust functionality and scalability, QuickBooks is an excellent choice for Caroline as she plans for future growth.

Intuit QuickBooks, a seasoned veteran in the accounting software realm, brings a wealth of experience and reliability to Caroline's financial management endeavors. With its powerful features and ability to adapt to evolving business needs, QuickBooks sets the stage for Caroline's ambitious growth plans.

Pros:

- Comprehensive accounting features, including invoicing, expense tracking, and tax preparation
- Robust reporting capabilities for deep financial analysis
- Integration with numerous third-party applications, allowing for enhanced functionality
- User-friendly interface with ample resources and customer support
- Mobile app for convenient financial management on the go

Cons:

- Steeper learning curve for users unfamiliar with accounting concepts
- Relatively expensive higher-tier pricing plans

Kashoo:

Kashoo caters specifically to the needs of small businesses and freelancers, offering a seamless blend of simplicity and robust features. With Kashoo, Caroline can effortlessly handle her finances, track expenses, generate professional invoices, and gain valuable insights while enjoying a user-friendly interface that doesn't compromise functionality.

Pros:

- Intuitive and easy-to-use interface, perfect for users with limited accounting knowledge
- Robust invoicing capabilities, including recurring invoices and online payment options
- Real-time financial reports for accurate insights into business performance
- Integration with popular payment gateways for seamless transaction processing
- Affordable pricing plans tailored for small businesses

Cons:

- Limited advanced features compared to more robust accounting software
- Less extensive customer support

Melio:

Melio offers a unique twist to traditional accounting software by focusing on simplifying and digitizing business payments. With Melio, Caroline can manage all her vendor payments, keep track of due dates, and even pay bills using a single platform, streamlining her financial transactions.

Melio transforms Caroline's financial landscape by introducing a streamlined platform that simplifies vendor payments and bill management. With Melio, Caroline gains the power to handle transactions effortlessly, stay organized, and never miss a due date—all within a convenient platform.

Pros:

- Streamlined vendor payment management, allowing for easy scheduling and tracking
- Integration with major accounting software for seamless financial synchronization
- Option to pay vendors using bank transfers or credit cards
- User-friendly interface with straightforward navigation
- Free to use for basic payment functionalities

Cons:

- Limited features beyond vendor payments and bill management
- Paid subscription required for some advanced functionalities

Patriot Software Accounting:

Patriot Software Accounting is an all-in-one accounting solution that offers comprehensive features for small businesses. With its emphasis on simplicity and affordability, Patriot Software Accounting is a strong contender for Caroline's financial management needs.

Patriot Software Accounting emerges as a reliable ally for Caroline's financial management journey, combining comprehensive features with an emphasis on simplicity and affordability, making it a formidable candidate to meet her business's accounting needs quickly.

Pros:

- Easy-to-use interface, making it ideal for users with limited accounting experience

- Full-featured accounting capabilities, including invoicing, expense tracking, and payroll
- Affordable pricing plans designed for small businesses
- Excellent customer support with live chat and phone options
- Cloud-based accessibility for convenient financial management

Cons:
- Somewhat limited advanced reporting options compared to more robust accounting software
- Separate subscription for payroll features

NetSuite

NetSuite's Enterprise Resource Planning (ERP) is a must-have accounting tool allowing small businesses to create a perfectly baked financial operation. The platform offers users access to an extensive selection of financial ingredients like financial management, accounts payable, order management, fulfillment, receivable modules, and procurement.

With NetSuite, small business owners like Caroline can weigh and track their expenses, revenue, and assets (remember these keywords? If not, you can take a quick look at the earlier chapters) to create a balanced financial recipe. The innovative tool allows you to streamline your financial processes and automates repetitive accounting procedures to achieve a balanced financial outcome.

Pros
- Offers a diverse set of financial accounting tools
- Ideal for small and large businesses
- Cloud-based, thus offering ease of access
- Provides third-party integrations

Cons
- Costly
- Limited customization
- Poor customer support

Sage Business Cloud Accounting

If you're new to the world of accounting, Sage Business Cloud Accounting is your one-stop solution to all financial accounting problems. This innovative platform offers users a wide range of state-of-the-art features.

With Sage, you can send and track invoices and payments, unlock a user-friendly design, and simplify complex accounting procedures. What's more, the state-of-the-art tool safeguards confidential financial data with security measures, thus protecting it from intruders and potential threats.

Pros
- Offers an intuitive and user-friendly interface
- Cost-effective and accessible
- Streamlines invoicing and payment management
- Provides innovative third-party integrations

Cons
- Limited customization options
- Reporting limitations
- Poor scalability and customer support

Truly Small Accounting

Truly Small Accounting is the secret ingredient small businesses need to create a successful financial recipe. This innovative and reliable platform allows users to measure and track financial transactions, ensuring the ideal balance of revenue and expenses.

It handles financial functions like contact management, bills, invoices, expense tracking, and bank reconciliation. With its user-friendly interface and insightful reports, Caroline can monitor and enhance financial performance.

Pros

- Exceptional user experience
- Intuitive and user-friendly design
- Easy-to-understand transaction and contact management
- Innovative invoice creation and payment tracking tools

Cons

- Overpriced
- No product and service records
- Zero invoice customization

Xero

Xero is a dynamic and innovative accounting software that helps track and measure financial transactions, maintain excellent supplier relationships, and minimize the risks of costly late fees.

Xero also seamlessly combines multiple financial ingredients, including expense tracking, invoicing, bookkeeping, and bank reconciliation. The revolutionary platform also offers a customizable dashboard to review invoices and access insights.

Pros

- Access to a user-friendly and intuitive interface
- Numerous third-party integrations
- Automatic and seamless bank reconciliation
- Collaborative working environment

Cons

- Limited customizations
- Comparatively expensive
- Lacks advanced features

Wave

Wave is a free yet effective accounting software helping small businesses and freelancers. With this state-of-the-art cloud-based platform, you can create accurate measurements and track financial transactions. In addition, Wave's user-friendly and intuitive interface provides small businesses with step-by-step guidance and tutorials. The innovative software also offers detailed reports and in-depth insights to help users monitor their financial performance and improve their financial performance.

Pros

- Free to use and accessible
- User-friendly interface that's easy to navigate
- Seamless invoicing and payment management

Cons

- Limited features due to free access
- Poor customer support
- Comparatively less third-party integrations
- Not suitable for large and growing businesses

Comparison Table: Everything You Need to Know About the Best Accounting Software

Accounting Software	Invo icing	Expense Tracking	Scala bility	Custo mizati on	Multi-User Access (Collabor ation)	Inventory Managem ent	Pricing
FreshBooks	Yes	Yes	Limit ed	Limit ed	No	No	Starts at $15/mo
Intuit QuickBooks	Yes	Yes	Yes	Yes	Yes	Yes	Starts at $25/mo
Kashoo	Yes	Yes	Limit ed	Limit ed	Yes	No	Starts at $19.95/mo
Melio	Yes	Yes	No	No	Yes	No	Free but charges for additional features
Patriot Software Accounting	Yes	Yes	Yes	Yes	Yes	Yes	Starts at $15/mo
NetSuite	Yes	Yes	Yes	Yes	Yes	Yes	Pricing available on request
Sage Business Cloud Accounting	Yes	Yes	Yes	Yes	Yes	Yes	Pricing available on request
Truly Small Accounting	Yes	Yes	Limit ed	Limit ed	No	No	Starts at $12/mo
Xero	Yes	Yes	Yes	Yes	Yes	No	Starts at $11/mo
Wave	Yes	Yes	Yes	Limit ed	No	No	Free but charges for additional features

Now that we've learned everything about the wondrous world of accounting software, it's time to get our hands a little dirty! Let's move onto the fun part, aka the exercises and examples.

Test Your Knowledge: Fun Exercises, Examples, and Tips Questions

Q1. Caroline is ready to transform her financial management and transactions from so-so to world-class. But before she can do that, she needs to identify which accounting software is perfect for her. Which of the above-mentioned accounting platform do you think is perfect for the Sweet Caroline Bakery and why?

Response:

Q2. Take a look at the following table:

Accounting Software	Features
Freshbooks	Invoicing Expense tracking Bank reconciliation
Intuit Quickbooks	Invoicing Expense tracking Time tracking
Kashoo	Invoicing Expense tracking Multi-currency support
Melio	Invoicing Bill Payments Vendor Management
Patriot Software Accounting	Invoicing Expense tracking Payroll management
NetSuite	Scalable and comprehensive accounting Inventory management Multi-user access
Sage Business Cloud Accounting	Comprehensive accounting functionality Customization options Multi-user access
Truly Small Accounting	Intuitive interface Invoicing Expense tracking
Wave	Invoicing Expense Tracking Bank Reconciliation
Xero	User-friendly interface Invoicing Expense tracking

Now use this list of features to identify which of them helps make financial accounting a piece of cake.

Response:

Short Questions

Q1. What is accounting software? Explain in two to three sentences.

Response:

Q2. What are the benefits of accounting software?

Response:

Q3. Do you think cloud-based or desktop accounting software is better?

Response:

Q4. Can you integrate accounting software with other financial or business tools?

Response:

Q5. From the information discussed above, do you believe accounting software is expensive?

Response:

Multiple-Choice Questions

Tick the appropriate answers (you can check if you're right at the bottom):

Q1. Accounting software is designed to help small businesses manage:

a) Marketing and advertising
b) Inventory management
c) Online shopping
d) Bookkeeping

Q2. A primary feature of accounting software is:

a) Digital media marketing
b) Project management
c) Invoicing
d) Customer relationship management

Q3. Cloud-based accounting software allows businesses to access their financial data from:

a) Offline only on desktops
b) Any device with an Internet connection
c) A specific laptop
d) During business hours

Q4. The benefit of accounting software is that it:

a) Increases manual errors
b) Improves marketing capabilities
c) Streamlines tax compliance

d) Limits financial reporting and performance

Q5. Integration with third-party business and financial accounting tools helps:

a) Slow down the computer
b) Limit functionality
c) Automate repetitive tasks
d) Increase data security

True/False

Choose between true and false and mark the appropriate answer (don't just guess!):

Q1. Accounting software is designed to help identify areas for cost savings.

True   False

Q2. Accounting software entirely eliminates human involvement from the accounting processes.

True   False

Q3. Accounting software does sometimes offer payroll processing capabilities.

True   False

Q4. Multi-user access allows multiple users to work within the same system at the same time.

True   False

Q5. Inventory management is a feature primarily used by manufacturing businesses, never by accounting software.

True   False

Answers

Q1. Only Caroline knows for sure which accounting software suits her unique business (and baking) needs, but we can make a guess. She might choose Xero or Wave since they both offer essential financial accounting features like invoicing, expense tracking, bank reconciliation, scalability, and more. Besides this, Wave is free, which helps Caroline save costs, whereas Xero is scalable and customizable, which ensures that the software will grow as her business does.

Q2. Based on the list of features provided, the following features are essential for financial accounting.

Invoicing- This feature is offered by Freshbooks, Intuit Quickbooks, Kashoo, Melio, Patriot Software Accounting, Sage Business Cloud Accounting, Truly Small Accounting, Wave, and Xero. With this robust feature, business owners can generate and send professional and accurate invoices within seconds.

Expense Tracking- This feature is offered by Freshbooks, Intuit Quickbooks, Kashoo, Patriot Software Accounting, Truly Small Accounting, Wave, and Xero. With this feature, businesses can record and categorize business expenses to simplify monitoring and managing a company's outflows.

Bank Reconciliation- Freshbooks, Kashoo, and Wave provide bank reconciliation features. This tool allows users to match recorded transactions with bank statements to minimize discrepancies and ensure accuracy.

Time Tracking- Although only Intuit Quickbooks offers time tracking, this tool is beneficial for businesses that bill clients hourly or those who need to monitor employee productivity.

Vendor Management- This feature is only offered by Melio, but it is essential for keeping track of suppliers and their contact information, thus making it easier for you to manage and maintain business relationships.

Payroll Management- This feature is exclusively offered by Patriot Software Accounting and is helpful for handling and streamlining employee wages, taxes, and other payroll-related tasks. This feature is ideal for large businesses that have to manage large sums of money.

Scalable and Comprehensive Accounting- Netsuite offers scalable and comprehensive accounting capabilities for growing businesses. With this feature, companies can go beyond bookkeeping and unlock inventory management and multi-user access.

Multi-User Access- NetSuite, Sage Business Cloud Accounting, and Truly Small Accounting offer multi-user access, which helps multiple team members and accountants join and collaborate on software simultaneously.

Intuitive Interface- Truly Small Accounting and Xero offer an exceptionally user-friendly and intuitive interface, which makes navigating and utilizing them super straightforward. Thus, these tools are ideal for beginners.

Short Answers

Q1. Accounting software is a computer program for assisting businesses in managing and improving financial transactions. It also helps to record income and expenses, track inventory, and generate invoices.

Q2. The benefits of accounting software include improving efficiency and performance, minimizing repetitive tasks, reducing errors, and providing real-time financial information.

Q3. The choice for cloud-based or desktop accounting software depends on accessibility, collaboration requirements, customization needs, data control, and safety precautions. While cloud-based software offer flexibility, remote control, and data safety, desktop-based tools promise more data control and customization options.

Q4. Yes, accounting software provides multiple third-party integrations and collaborations, such as CRM systems, payment processors, project management software, and e-commerce platforms.

Q5. Since the cost of accounting software varies based on the provider, features, third-party integrations, and number of users, there's no one-size-fits-all answer to this question.

Multiple-Choice

Q1. d

Q2. c

Q3. b

Q4. c

Q5. c

True/False

Q1. True

Q2. False

Q3. True

Q4. True

Q5. False

Tips

- Set your accounting software budget ahead of time. Ensure you include the cost of training and installation as well.
- Remember to test your accounting software options before making a final option. That way, you and other people involved in accounting tasks can make the ideal choice for your business.
- Before you make a final choice, consider identifying which financial accounting features best match your needs. Once you jot down your business's unique needs, you can find accounting software that suits your requirements and helps you hit your goals.

Great, we've reached the very end of this chapter! Here's a meringue pie to help you celebrate your win and hard work. Now get ready for the next chapter, where we'll dive into the secrets of finding and hiring the perfect accountant!

CHAPTER 10

Unlocking Financial Success: Hiring and Choosing the Right Accountant

As Caroline's business grows and thrives, she faces the challenge of managing her expanding financial responsibilities. While she has diligently handled her accounting tasks thus far, she realizes that the time has come to consider enlisting the support of a professional accountant. By doing so, Caroline aims to free up her valuable time and expertise, allowing her to focus on what she does best: managing and growing her business.

Behold, dear reader, the time has come to unlock the secrets of hiring an accountant and exploring the riveting factors that Caroline needs to consider when making this oh-so critical decision. From understanding when it's the right time to bring her accountant sidekick on board to the process of selecting the perfect financial partner for her business, Caroline will gain valuable insights to navigate this important step.

Caroline recognizes that entrusting her financial matters to a qualified and experienced accountant can unlock new levels of efficiency, accuracy, and financial success. An accountant can provide expert guidance, ensure compliance with tax regulations, offer strategic financial advice, and handle complex accounting tasks. By availing herself of professional accounting services, Caroline can streamline her financial processes, better understand her business' financial health, and make well-informed decisions that drive growth and profitability.

Together, we will explore the pathways to finding a financial partner who will navigate the intricacies of numbers, allowing Caroline to focus her energy on what truly matters—her business's continued success and growth. Let us explore the captivating world of hiring and choosing the right accountant. Who will it be, the wise old owl with an aversion to computers? The shiny new penny, armed with the latest accounting software? Or a hip middle-ground hero, at home both with ledgers and laptops? The suspense is mind-numbing.

The Importance of Hiring an Accountant

Having a knowledgeable and skilled accountant by your side can be a game-changer in the fast-paced business world. An accountant brings a wealth of expertise and financial acumen that can help propel your business toward success. From providing valuable financial insights to ensuring compliance with tax regulations, an accountant is crucial in maximizing profitability, minimizing risks, and making informed strategic decisions.

Caroline understands the significance of hiring an accountant in her quest for financial success. She can tap into their specialized knowledge with their guidance, allowing her to focus on core business operations. By working closely with an accountant, Caroline can better understand her financial position, receive tailored advice, and make informed decisions that drive growth and profitability. Additionally, an accountant can provide Caroline with peace of mind, knowing that her financial matters are in capable hands and enabling her to navigate the complexities of the business world.

Understanding the Optimal Time to Hire an Accountant

Like many business owners, Caroline understands the importance of delegating accounting tasks to a professional. By hiring an accountant, she can offload the burden of financial management and focus on the core aspects of running her business.

Managing the financial aspects of a business can be a complex and demanding task. As an entrepreneur, it's essential to recognize when it's the right time to bring in the expertise of an accountant to ensure the smooth operation and growth of your venture. By understanding the optimal times to hire an accountant, you can make informed decisions that will benefit your business in the long run.

Knowing when to hire an accountant is crucial for maximizing efficiency and ensuring accurate financial management. Let's explore some critical scenarios where bringing in an accountant can make a significant difference.

Starting a Business
Caroline needs an accountant to help her set up her financial framework, including choosing the ideal business structure, creating a budget, and selecting an effective accounting system.

Tax Preparation
Accountants know the ins and outs of tax preparation. Since they have a deep understanding of tax laws, compliances, and regulations, they can help you create successful and accurate tax returns. Accountants can also aid in identifying tax

deductions and credits to maximize tax savings and minimize audit risks. The result is that Caroline stays compliant while growing her business.

Financial Analysis
Accountants review your financial statements, ratios, and key performance indicators (KPIs) to determine how you maintain your business's financial health. In addition, accountants can help identify cost-saving opportunities and strategies to enhance profitability.

Bookkeeping
Bookkeeping is the building block of tracking and enhancing your business's financial health. If you're anything like Caroline and tend to misplace your business records, an accountant can help you organize receipts, invoices, and other financial documents.

Furthermore, an accountant helps ensure all your records are accurate and up to date to help balance your financial ingredients, generate killer reports, reconcile accounts, and promote a clear understanding of your business's financial health and position.

Audit Preparation
Just like how Caroline's bakery undergoes occasional inspections, businesses may face audits from tax authorities and auditors. We know, scary! But with an accountant, you don't have to worry about unexpected tax authorities.

Accountants help ensure all your records are well-organized and readily available when needed to create your financial statements (which we learned *all* about in the previous chapters).

Moreover, a reliable and expert accountant can help you navigate the audit process, ensuring zero risk of penalties and a 100 percent ability to focus on priority tasks.

Unlocking Business Success: How to Find the Perfect Accountant to Run Your Finances Efficiently

Just like no two bakeries share the same taste and texture of a chocolate cake, no two accountants boast the same capabilities and experience. For this reason, it's important for you to assess your needs and compare different experts to identify whether they suit your needs.

Before you sigh and give up, this step is super easy! Let's break down the key factors you need to consider to ensure financial success.

Qualifications

Just like Caroline would never hire a new baker without analyzing their training, certifications, experience, and skill set, you should never partner with an accountant lacking the necessary qualifications.

So before you hire an accountant to help flourish your business, identify whether they have the necessary certifications (like a chartered accountant). That way, you can determine whether they meet the professional standards and have the necessary credentials.

Specialization

An accountant who specializes in large manufacturing doesn't have the experience and expertise to deal with Caroline's bakery and its unique financial challenges. So to ensure maximum efficiency, Caroline needs to contact an accountant with industry-specific knowledge to minimize the risks of fines, unlock customized solutions, and optimize financial performance.

Besides this, working with an accountant with specialized expertise can help Caroline access targeted advice and avoid roadblocks that can hurt her business's performance.

Communication

Effective communication is the yeast of your financial operations, ensuring it rises smoothly. Businesses need accountants who can communicate quickly and effectively. Ideally, you should seek an accountant who actively listens to your concerns, understands your goals, and offers insightful guidance. Remember, transparent and open communication between you and your accountant is the secret ingredient for your financial success.

Compatibility

Partnering with an accountant with whom you feel comfortable is necessary for building an effective and long-term relationship. It's best to schedule a consultation or interview to assess how well you connect with them and whether they align with your business's value.

Availability

Just like Caroline relies on her baker to be accessible during work hours, she needs an accountant who can handle her workload and is available when needed. Since Caroline can't read minds, she needs to inquire and discuss their availability for meetings, working hours, and ability to respond to time-sensitive tasks.

Fees

Similarly, as Caroline can't kick start a new baking project without considering the cost of ingredients, you can't hire an accountant without inquiring about their fee structure to identify whether they fit your budget.

Many accountants charge an hourly rate, whereas others offer a fixed fee. So discuss your desired accountant's billing terms before you partner up.

Yay! We've made it to the end of Chapter 10, which means you now officially know all the basics of hiring an accountant to measure and enhance your business's financial performance. The next step is to jump into some fun and exciting exercises and examples. Let's go!

Test Your Knowledge: Fun Exercises, Examples, and Tips
Questions

Q1. Take a look at the following table comprising basic information about three accountants in Caroline's vicinity:

Accountant	Communication Skills	Financial Analysis Expertise	Industry Experience	Problem-Solving and Time-Sensitive Abilities	Fees (Cost)
Barry Johnson	Moderate	Moderate	High	High	$150/hour
Sarah Smith	Good	High	Moderate	High	$120/hour
Phil Dendy	Excellent	High	Moderate	High	$180/hour

Based on this information (excluding budget considerations), which of the three accountants do you believe would be the best fit for Sweet Caroline Bakery and why?

Response:

Q2. As an owner of a small bakery in her hometown, Caroline needs an accountant to manage her financial operations. But before she can get started, she needs to identify the factors she should consider to find the perfect fit for her business. Describe in detail the different considerations a bakery owner should know when entering the accountant hiring market:

Response:

Short Questions

Answer the following questions in two to three lines:

Q1. Why is hiring an accountant essential for businesses?

Response:

Q2. How can an accountant benefit a small business like Sweet Caroline Bakery?

Response:

Q3. Should you hire an accountant with industry-specific experience?

Response:

Q4. How do you find the perfect accountant for your small or mid-sized business?

Response:

Q5. When seeking an accountant, should you ensure they're up to date with tax laws within your industry or not?

Response:

Multiple-Choice Questions

Q1. What is the primary role of an accountant in a business?

a) Managing inventory
b) Financial reporting and analysis
c) Sales and marketing
d) Human resources management

Q2. What is the significance of qualifications when choosing an accountant?

a) It ensures extensive knowledge of tax laws in all industries
b) It guarantees they can handle any accounting task
c) It confirms they meet the professional standards

d) It is irrelevant to their ability to perform accounting tasks

Q3. Which of the following factors should you consider when assessing an accountant?

a) How well they speak
b) Whether they can market
c) Technical accounting knowledge
d) Budgeting

Q4. Why should businesses conduct interviews when hiring an accountant?

a) To assess their technical accounting knowledge
b) To identify their athleticism
c) To learn about their artistic skills
d) To determine their musical talent

Q5. What is the significance of compatibility when choosing an accountant for your business?

a) It ensures they have a similar personality as yours
b) It guarantees they will follow your every order and never make a mistake
c) It promotes effective communication and collaboration
d) It allows them to work independently without needing input

True/False

Q1. Industry-specific knowledge does not matter when hiring an accountant.

        True   False

Q2. Communication skills and collaboration do not matter when assessing abilities.

<table>
<tr><td align="center">True</td><td align="center">False</td></tr>
</table>

Q3. Attention to detail is an important skill for accountants to effectively analyze financial data.

<table>
<tr><td align="center">True</td><td align="center">False</td></tr>
</table>

Q4. An accountant needs culinary arts knowledge to excel.

<table>
<tr><td align="center">True</td><td align="center">False</td></tr>
</table>

Q5. You must assess an accountant's knowledge of accounting software and technology.

<table>
<tr><td align="center">True</td><td align="center">False</td></tr>
</table>

Answers:

Q1. Based on the provided information, Phil Dendy is the best fit for Sweet Caroline Bakery. This is because he has excellent communication skills, which are essential for ensuring the accountant effectively understands and conveys financial information to Caroline and her stakeholders. In addition, Phil has moderate industry experience, indicating he has a solid understanding of the challenges specific to a bakery and can provide tailored guidance to solve potential financial problems faced by Sweet Caroline Bakery. Lastly, Phil has high problem-solving skills and can quickly solve time-sensitive tasks. This is crucial for addressing any financial issues and obstacles Caroline's bakery may encounter and finding effective and efficient financial solutions to overcome them. Sarah Smith could be an alternate choice if fit is good and budget is of greater concern.

Q2. When hiring an accountant for Sweet Caroline Bakery, Caroline should consider several crucial factors to ensure she finds the perfect candidate for handling her financial operations. Here are the essential considerations.

- **Qualification-** Before hiring any accountant, it's essential to identify whether they possess the training, skills, certifications, and experience to handle a bakery.
- **Specialization-** Caroline should seek an accountant with in-depth industry knowledge and experience to ensure maximum efficiency. That way, they can quickly solve bakery-specific financial challenges.
- **Communication-** Effective communication and collaboration are crucial for ensuring transparency between the two parties, building trust, and ensuring the accountant works well with the other departments of Sweet Caroline Bakery.
- **Availability-** When hiring an accountant, Caroline must ensure that the accountant can respond to her inquiries in a timely fashion. Besides this, she may need to discuss working hours and their ability to solve time-sensitive tasks.
- **Compatibility-** Compatibility between Caroline and her accountant is essential to running efficient financial operations and a successful bakery. So when hiring, she should identify whether the accountant shares her values and understands her unique business goals.
- **Fees-** Lastly, Caroline needs to consider her desired accountant's fees and billing structure. Based on her budget, she might prefer one who works hourly or monthly. Caroline needs to check her listed candidate's fee structure to identify who best fits

within her budget and whether there are any hidden fees.

Short Answers

Q1. Hiring an accountant is important because they offer expertise in financial management, tax compliance, and strategic decision-making. With the help of an accountant, businesses can ensure accurate report-keeping, maximize tax savings, and unlock valuable business insights for long-term success.

Q2. An accountant can offer various benefits to a small business such as Sweet Caroline Bakery by offering essential and tailored financial services like bookkeeping, tax preparations, financial analysis, expert solutions, and strategic planning. Besides this, they can help small businesses manage their finances, ensure compliance, and unlock expert advice.

Q3. It's generally best to hire an accountant with industry-specific experience. These accountants will be familiar with the unique financial challenges faced by your business and have a deep understanding of the related rules and regulations. Therefore, because of their specialized knowledge, they can provide you with tailored advice and support to ensure business growth and profitability.

Q4. Finding the perfect accountant for small or mid-sized businesses involves defining your needs, seeking referrals, conducting in-depth interviews, assessing qualifications and experience, and considering compatibility and communication.

Q5. Yes, it is crucial to ensure your desired financial accountant is up to date with tax laws within your industry.

Industry-specific knowledge helps them navigate specific tax requirements, ensure compliance, and optimize tax planning.

Multiple-Choice

Q1. b

Q2. c

Q3. c

Q4. a

Q5. c

True/False

Q1. False

Q2. False

Q3. True

Q4. False

Q5. True

Tips

- Select an accountant who will go beyond just crunching the numbers and will help your business achieve its goals.
- Make sure you find an accountant who has experience working with small businesses and go with your gut.
- Remember to conduct thorough interviews and review client testimonials before hiring an accountant

Congratulations, you've reached the end of the last chapter! Here's a pastry *and* candy to celebrate your newly-found knowledge of financial accounting. Finish them up quickly, for we're about to wrap up this exciting journey!

CONCLUSION

Wrapping It All Up : Becoming a Confident Small Business Owner

Just like a junior baker learning the art of baking mouthwatering and delightful confections, Caroline's journey to learning the basics of financial accounting has equipped her with the necessary ingredients to ensure the sweet success of a growing small-town bakery. As she reflects on her newfound knowledge, she realizes how understanding the fundamentals of accounting can impact all her business ventures, allowing her to transform into her town's most famous bakery!

By reading this book, Caroline was able to create a foundation in financial accounting, which paved the way for her small business's success. Moreover, by grasping accounting knowledge and uncovering the secrets to keeping meticulous records of expenses, revenues, and profits, Caroline can whisk away financial uncertainty, allowing her to create a perfectly baked business mix!

But it's not all about crunching numbers, counting the dough, and getting the bread! Armed with her newfound and in-depth knowledge of accounting, Caroline can make smart business decisions like a baking expert selecting the finest ingredients to create their next delectable treat. Moreover, analyzing financial data allows her to sprinkle her business with a dash of sweet opportunities and an extra frosting of success, ensuring there's little risk of sour surprises.

And let's not forget the sprinkles and decorations that add a little something to Caroline's financial cake—cash flow management! Having uncovered the basics of cash flow management, Caroline can now keep a watchful and skeptical eye on her bakery's inflows and outflows, just like she manages her pantry. With this newly learned skill, Caroline can keep her business's oven running hot and her dreams rising like freshly baked bread.

Through her exciting accounting journey, Caroline has discovered a hidden treasure of fun and essential accounting words, from assets and liabilities to revenue and expenses. Learning these terms, their role in her business, and their overall importance has empowered Caroline, and she feels like a seasoned business owner. Now when she discusses her business's not so complex financial concoctions with her accountant, business investors, and stakeholders, she feels confident and at home back in her financial kitchen.

What's more? The financial statements, aka the flour to Caroline's baking cake: she can now read them like her baking recipe, making it easy for her to assess the health of her business with a keen eye. It's like taste-testing her business's batter to identify the perfect baking time, allowing her to gauge and adjust her business's performance accordingly.

And what about the budgeting and forecasting skills Caroline picked up during her accounting journey? Like a master chef who plans the baking and decoration ahead, she can now plan ahead, set financial goals, and anticipate the rise and growth of her business—just like her recipes indicate when the soufflé will puff, she now has the perfect recipe for success.

Furthermore, learning the basics of financial accounting ensures that she stays compliant with taxes. That's just like keeping the kitchen clean and tidy to ensure zero mess and stress. Caroline can now follow all the rules and regulations, ensuring that her business stays as fresh and smart as her perfectly baked goods. She also knows how and which accounting software to use, just like every bakery needs a trusty sous chef to ensure the quality and deliciousness of their treats.

With this awesome software, she can organize her financial ingredients, reducing the risk of errors and allowing her to focus on the creative side of her business. But like every master baker knows the value of expert advice, Caroline needs an accountant to unlock their wisdom and expertise to create the perfect blend of financial flavors, ensuring her business rises to new heights.

As she concludes her accounting journey, Caroline's prowess inspires her to blend together her new financial knowledge to create an unbeatable business foundation and manage her money matters with ease. From learning the intricacies of financial statements and reports to speaking the language of accounting, she's all set to create her very own recipe for sweet, sweet success.

But her journey doesn't end here. As Caroline confidently moves forward, she discovers the power of accounting to develop future growth plans. Just like a baker envisioning new and delicious treats, Caroline now has the knowledge to lay out a roadmap for her business's growth and expansion. Having learned the secrets to financial analysis, she can now identify potential growth opportunities to capture new markets and take her bakery to brand-new heights.

Now that she can *talk the talk* with her accountant just as confidently as she discusses the perfect balance of flavors with her peers, she can clearly communicate her business's financial goals and achieve milestones to bake the perfect recipe for financial success. Caroline's accounting journey has also taught her the importance of understanding financial accounting, setting her up for future learning while allowing her to make strategic adjustments to fine-tune her operations for maximum efficiency, just like baking and savoring the entire rise of a mouth-watering dessert buffet.

Overall, Caroline's accounting journey has allowed her to transform her small business aspirations into a delightful reality. Like a bakery owner with a secret recipe, she now possesses the knowledge and skills to navigate the entrepreneurship sphere with confidence. She can also use her accounting prowess to develop future growth plans to create a culinary masterpiece.

If you're an aspiring entrepreneur, follow Caroline's footsteps to discover the secret ingredients to business success. Just as she measures her ingredients to perfection, you can use accounting knowledge to track income and expenses with precision to create a clear financial picture. Moreover, you can empower yourself to develop impressive growth strategies while ensuring compliance with tax laws.

With accounting as your trusty recipe, you can navigate the challenges and risks of entrepreneurship, creating a powerful foundation for your small business and a deliciously prosperous future. Now that you've reached the end of this book, you now know that accounting is more than numbers— it's the door that leads to your business dreams. So grab your apron, tie your hair back, and get ready to whip up business success. Bon appétit!

Tips

Before you close this book, we've got a few more tips you can walk away with:

- Keep this book handy so you can easily review the key concepts you have recently learned and mastered. p.s. There's a comprehensive glossary at the back of this book.
- Use the resources and advice we've added for continued learning and growth in small business accounting, including taking industry-specific workshops and online courses, joining professional associations, networking with like-minded small business owners, and reading similar books.
- Test your newly learned knowledge with fun quizzes and interactive exercises (like the ones in the chapters you completed) to revise and reinforce your financial accounting skills.

You got this!

References

[1]Small Business Owners & Cash Flow Uncertainty | QuickBooks Canada. (2022, February 18). https://quickbooks.intuit.com/ca/resources/cash-flow/cash-flow-uncertainty/

[2] Houston, M. (2020, December 22). How This Cash Collector Turns Outdated Accounts Into Cash Quickly. *Forbes*. https://www.forbes.com/sites/melissahouston/2020/12/22/how-this-cash-collector-turns-outdated-accounts-into-cash-quickly/

[3],[4]"2019 Small Business Finance and HR Report," *OnPay*. https://onpay.com/hr/basics/2019-small-business-finance-hr

[5] *12 fun and interesting facts about accounting*. (2022, February 11). https://contentsnare.com/fun-facts-about-accounting/

[6] Consult, L. (2022, August 25). *5 fun facts about accounting*. Lead Consult. https://leadconsult-bg.com/en/5-fun-facts-about-accounting/

Resources

- **Small Business Administration** is a great resource for small businesses. They offer many resources, including:
  - Business planning tools
  - Financing
  - Government contracts
  - Online resources
- **SCORE** is a non-profit organization that provides free mentoring and advice to small businesses, as well as many free templates for small businesses.
- **Fundera** offers a free service that compares small business loans from different lenders.
- **LegalZoom** is a website that provides legal services, including business structure.
- **NOLO** is another website that provides legal information and resources.

Accounting Standards:

- **FASB (Financial Accounting Standards Board)** is the private-sector organization that sets standards in US. Their site has some free resources. It also contains the ASU (Accounting Standards Update) which are US standards updates issued by FASB.
- **IASB (International Accounting Standards Board)** is the private-sector organization that sets standards internationally. Their site also has free resources.

- **IFRS (International Financial Reporting Standards)** is an organization that provides free access to all international financial reporting standards (issued by IASB).

Financials/Ratios:

- **QuickBooks Online** is a cloud-based accounting software that offers a free trial, and you can access financial statement resources.
- **FreshBooks** is an online accounting software that offers free templates.
- **Canva** is a graphic design software that offers free financial templates for presentations.
- **Investopedia** is a website that provides financial education and information, including calculators and tutorials on financial ratios.

Financial Risks/Challenges:

- **NFIB (National Federation of Independent Business)** is a non-profit organization that represents small businesses in the US and includes free resources on their website.
- **AICPA (American Institute of Certified Public Accountants)** is a professional organization by accountants that provides free resources for small businesses on their website.

Fraud:

- **FTC (Federal Trade Commission)** is a government agency that protects consumers from fraud. Their website includes resources on fraud prevention for small businesses.

- **NSBA (National Small Business Association)** is a non-profit organizations that represents small businesses in the US and includes resources for fraud prevention for small businesses on their website.
- **NCSA (National Cyber Security Alliance)** is a non-profit organization that promotes cyber security awareness and has resources and checklists for small business fraud prevention.

Budgeting & Forecasting:

- **Microsoft Excel Video Training** – Microsoft has some free online courses for Excel.
- **Learnopoly (Learnopoly-Excel)** offers a list of various Microsoft Excel courses available on different websites (primarily paid).
- **SCORE, Quickbooks Online and Freshbooks** also offer free budgeting templates.

Taxes and Compliance:

- **IRS**– The IRS website is a great resource for tax and compliance information.
- **Check with your state or local government** – they offer free resources.

There are various online tax preparation websites, but I recommend you utilize a professional preparer for your small business.

Accounting Software:

- FreshBooks
- Intuit QuickBooks
- Kashoo

- Melio
- Patriot Software Accounting
- NetSuite
- Sage Business Cloud Accounting
- Truly Small Accounting
- Wave
- Xero

Hiring an Accountant

- **AICPA-CIMA Global Career Hub**– dedicated accounting job board of the AICPA-CIMA. It features international recruitment as well.
- **iHireAccounting**– recruitment resource for employers and job seekers in the finance and accounting industry
- **Indeed**– a free job posting site available in over 60 countries and currently most visited job site in the US

Glossary

- **Accounting-** Recording, organizing, and analyzing financial transactions.
- **Accounts Payable-** The amounts owed by an organization to its suppliers and vendors for goods/services bought on credit but not paid.
- **Accounts Receivable-** The amount owed to a small business by its customers for goods/services sold on credit but not yet collected.
- **Accrual Accounting-** An accounting method where transactions are recorded when they occur, regardless of when the cash is exchanged, providing a more accurate representation of a small business's financial position.
- **Assets-** Resources owned by a business with economic value, like cash, inventory, and equipment.
- **Balance Sheet-** A financial statement displaying a business's assets, liabilities, and equity at a specific time.
- **Bookkeeping-** A fundamental aspect of accounting which that involves recording daily financial transactions, such as sales, expenses, and purchases, into the general ledger.
- **Cash Accounting-** An accounting method where transactions are recorded when cash is received or paid, making it ideal for small businesses with simpler financial structures.
- **Cash Flow-** The movement of cash in and out of business, including income, expenses, and investments.
- **Charts of Accounts (CoA)-** A systematic list of all accounts used by a small business to categorize financial transactions and streamline accounting processes.

- **Cost of Capital-** The average rate of return a small business must earn on its investments to maintain its capital structure's current value.
- **Cost of Goods Sold-** The direct expenses incurred to produce goods/services sold by a small business. It's also an essential component in determining gross profit.
- **Depreciation-** Allocating the cost of an asset over its useful life.
- **Dividends-** Any payment made by a small business to its shareholders as a distribution of its profits.
- **Equity-** The residual interest in the assets of a small business once you deduct the liabilities. It represents the business owner's claim on the company's assets.
- **Expenses-** Costs incurred by a business to generate revenue, e.g., rent, salaries, and utilities.
- **Financial Forecast-** An estimate of a business's future financial performance. It typically includes projected expenses and cash flow.
- **Financial Ratios-** Mathematical expressions used to analyze the small business's financial performance, such as profitability, liquidity, and solvency. It helps a business assess its overall health.
- **Financial Statement Analysis-** The process of evaluating a small business's financial statements to evaluate its performance, trends, and financial health, which facilitates smart decision-making.
- **Fiscal Year-** The accounting period predefined by a business for financial reporting. This does not need to coincide with the calendar year.
- **Fixed Assets-** Long-term tangible assets held by small businesses for investing in its operations, including buildings, land, vehicles, and machinery.

- **Income Statement-** Another word for Profit and Loss Statement, the Income Statement shows a summary of small business's revenues, expenses, and net income over a specific period. It indicates an organization's profitability.
- **Intangible Assets-** Non-physical assets with long-term values, such as copyrights, patents, trademarks, and goodwill.
- **Internal Controls-** Policies and regulations implemented by a small business to safeguard assets, prevent fraud, and ensure accurate financial reporting.
- **Inventory Management-** The process of tracking and controlling a small business's inventory levels to optimize stock levels and minimize carrying costs.
- **Liabilities-** Debts or obligations a business owes, like loans, accounts payable, and accrued expenses.
- **Liquidity-** The ability of a business to meet its short-term financial obligations without disrupting its operations.
- **Payroll-** The process of calculating and distributing employee wages and taxes, ensuring compliance with tax and labor laws and regulations.
- **Profit Margin-** A financial ratio for measuring a small business's profitability by expressing net profit as a percentage of total revenue.
- **Owner's Equity-** The portion of a business's assets belonging to the owners, such as retained earnings and contributed capital.
- **Return on Investment-** An important financial metric used to measure the profitability of an investment/project by comparing the net profit to the initial investment.
- **Revenue-** Revenue represents the business's earnings from various sources.

- **Solvency-** The ability of a business to meet its long-term financial obligations while demonstrating financial stability
- **Tax Credits-** Direct reductions in a small business's tax liability, which aids in incentivizing activities like hiring employees or investing in specific projects.
- **Tax Deductions-** Expenses that a small business subtracts from its taxable income to alleviate its tax liability.
- **Trial Balance-** A statement used to ensure that total debits equal total credits, resulting in accurate financial records.

Thank You

Dear Reader,

Before you close this book, I want to say a huge, huge thank you from the bottom of my heart for choosing to embark on this fun accounting journey with me! I sincerely hope you found value in this book and that it's become your close companion in your quest to conquer small business accounting.

As a token of my gratitude and to show my appreciation for your support, I've prepared a special gift just for you—a complete and free accounting checklist to continue your learning journey! Go here to download your free checklist.

https://dl.bookfunnel.com/jkjk5nrvta

If you had as much fun reading this book as I had while writing it, I'd be thrilled if you could take a few minutes from your busy schedule to leave a review on Amazon! Your honest feedback can help others discover and benefit from this. Please go here to review:

https://amzn.to/3PjaCZG

Once again, a big thank you for your support. I wish you all the best in your future business endeavors—trust me, you've got this!

With warmest regards,

Amy York

Author's Bio

Meet Amy, an experienced accounting professional with more than three decades of experience. She earned a bachelor's degree with honors in accounting and tackled the technological challenges of her career by earning a minor in computer science.

Amy advanced her career quickly, holding various management and executive roles along the way, including chief financial officer. However, when not crunching numbers or writing, she can usually be found curled up with a good book or watching some of her favorite shows. Amy also enjoys family time, traveling, the outdoors, and fussing over her beloved fur babies.

Amy's expertise in accounting and finance makes her an authority on the subject, but don't be intimidated! Amy can make accounting fun, engaging, and approachable. Her book on basic accounting promises to be an informative read that provides a view into finances for anyone wanting to increase their understanding. With Amy's guidance and passion for helping others, you will learn how to efficiently manage money while making informed financial decisions with greater ease and confidence.

Made in the USA
Monee, IL
29 November 2024

71601807R00144